Contents

How to use this book

This book provides three sets of exam papers that mirror the AQA GCSE exam papers.

The audio, teacher-examiner parts (for Paper 2: Speaking), model answers and mark schemes can be accessed using the QR codes throughout the book or by visiting http://www.oxfordsecondary.co.uk/aqagcse-spanish-pp.

The exam papers contain hints and tips. The first set of papers provides tips for all questions and all skills, in order to help you gain confidence in answering questions. In the second set of papers there are fewer tips for listening and reading. The third set of papers does not contain tips, so that you have an opportunity to practise answering questions independently in an exam situation.

AQA GCSE Spanish Foundation

AQA GCSE Spanish Foundation is made up of four exam papers, each with a weighting of 25% towards the final mark. The Foundation Tier is for students targeting Grades 1–5 and the Higher Tier is for students targeting Grades 4–9. For more details about the specification, please see the AQA website.

Paper 1: Listening

There are 35 minutes to complete the listening paper with 40 marks available. In Section A, the questions are in English and the answers required will either be non-verbal or in English. In Section B, the questions are in Spanish and the answers required will either be non-verbal or in Spanish.

The time includes 5 minutes at the start of the exam to read through the paper. Practise reading through the paper in this time. You may need to skim-read to get all the way through it, but try to use the time in a focused way. Identify the questions where you need to give several answers about the audio passage, or more than one piece of information, so that you're ready to listen out for the details you need. It's also good to read Section B carefully to make sure you understand the questions being asked.

The level of difficulty varies throughout the paper so don't lose heart if you encounter a hard question early on as it doesn't mean you will find the questions that follow even harder. In AQA GCSE Paper 1, there are some questions that appear both on the Foundation and Higher Tier papers.

Use the tips in the Set 1 and Set 2 listening papers in this book to build your confidence in exam technique and to help you listen out for the correct answers.

Paper 2: Speaking

There are 60 marks available for the Speaking paper. For Foundation Tier, you will have supervised preparation time of 12 minutes followed by an exam of 7–9 minutes.

There are three parts to the exam:

- Role-play (15 marks) – this will last approximately 2 minutes for Foundation Tier

- Photo card (15 marks) – this will last approximately 2 minutes for Foundation Tier

- General conversation (30 marks) – this will last between 3 and 5 minutes for Foundation Tier

The candidate chooses one theme for the general conversation and the other theme will be the one that hasn't been covered in the photo card. Here is a chart showing the possible test sequences based on the candidate's choice of theme:

Role-play	Candidate's chosen conversation theme	Photo card	Candidate's second conversation theme
1, 2 or 3	Theme 1: Identity and culture	B	Theme 3
		C	Theme 2
	Theme 2: Local, national, international and global areas of interest	A	Theme 3
		C	Theme 1
	Theme 3: Current and future study and employment	A	Theme 2
		B	Theme 1

Each paper in this book contains a role-play and a photo card from each theme. The teacher-examiner part and two marked model responses for each can be found online. For general conversation, there are two marked model responses included in the book for each paper, followed by tasks to complete:

- Set 1 covers Themes 2 and 1

- Set 2 covers Themes 2 and 3

- Set 3 covers Themes 1 and 3

There are two further general conversations with model answers online.

Tips are provided for the role-plays and photo cards in the Set 1 and Set 2 speaking papers in this book to help you respond more fully to the questions asked and anticipate the unexpected questions.

Paper 3: Reading

There are 45 minutes to complete the reading paper with 60 marks available. In Section A, the questions are in English and the answers required will either be non-verbal or in English. In Section B, the questions are in Spanish and the answers required will either be non-verbal or in Spanish. Different types of written language are used in the reading paper, including literary texts. In this book, example answers are given if further guidance is needed on how to answer a question, so watch out for these.

The level of difficulty varies throughout the paper so don't lose heart if you encounter a hard question early on as it doesn't mean you will find the questions that follow even harder. In AQA GCSE Paper 3, there are some questions that appear both on the Foundation and Higher Tier papers.

In Section C, there is a translation from Spanish into English with a minimum of 35 words.

Use the tips in the Set 1 and Set 2 reading papers in this book to build your confidence in exam technique and to help you pick out the correct answers from the text.

Paper 4: Writing

There is 1 hour to complete the writing paper with 50 marks available. All answers should be written in Spanish.

For Foundation Tier there are four questions:

- Question 1 (8 marks): this will require you to write four sentences about a photo.

- Question 2 (16 marks): 40 words are expected for this task, with a series of bullet points to cover in your response.

- Question 3 (10 marks): A translation from English into Spanish with a minimum of 35 words.

- Question 4 (16 marks): A choice of one from two structured writing tasks of 90 words with a series of bullet points to cover in your response. In AQA GCSE Paper 4, this question is the same as question 1 on the Higher Tier paper.

For Question 4, check whether you are required to use the familiar or polite 'you' form in your answer. In AQA GCSE Paper 4, this can vary from year to year, so you must read the instructions carefully.

Tips are provided in the Set 1 and Set 2 writing papers in this book, to help you respond to the questions and give guidance on extending your answers. Two marked model answers are included online for questions 2 and 4. Also included online are mark schemes for questions 1 and 3.

AQA GCSE Spanish (9-1)

F

Foundation Tier Paper 1 Listening

Time allowed: 35 minutes
(including 5 minutes' reading time before the test)

You will need no other materials.
The pauses are pre-recorded for this test.

Information
- The marks for the questions are shown in brackets. The maximum mark for this paper is 40.
- You must **not** use a dictionary.

Advice
This is what you should do for each item.
- After the question number is announced, there will be a pause to allow you to read the instructions and questions.
- Listen carefully to the recording and read the questions again.
- Listen to the recording again, and then answer the questions.
- When the next question is about to start you will hear a bleep.
- You may write at any time during the test.
- In **Section A**, answer the questions in **English**. In **Section B**, answer the questions in **Spanish**.
- You must answer all the questions in the spaces provided. Do not write on blank pages.
- Write neatly and put down all the information you are asked to give.
- **You must not ask questions or interrupt during the test.**
- You have five minutes to read through the question paper. You may make notes during this time. You may turn to the questions now.
- **The test starts now.**

Listen to the audio

Section A   Questions and answers in **English**

Helping the environment

While in Mexico, you listen to a podcast about the environment.

Which **two** things does each person mention?

Write the correct letters in the boxes.

> - Use your 5 minutes' reading time at the start of the exam to read the questions carefully and make notes.
> - From the multiple-choice answers, try to predict what kinds of words you might hear and eliminate the least likely answer(s) as soon as possible. For example, in these questions, *aire, animales, extinción, botellas* and *vehículos* are all key words.
> - This type of question also often benefits from a careful second listening.

0 1

A	Deforestation
B	Air pollution
C	Climate change
D	Endangered species

[ ]   [ ]

[2 marks]

0 2

A	Recycling
B	Saving water
C	Travelling responsibly
D	Volunteering

[ ]   [ ]

[2 marks]

School facilities

Your Spanish friend, Ernesto, is describing his school.

Answer in **English**.

What aspect does he **like** about the…

Example   canteen? <u>the food</u>

> - Read the instructions carefully and pay close attention to the example, if one is given, to make sure your answers provide the right level of detail. In this case, only a brief and succinct noun (i.e. '[the] food') is required for each answer. Realising this makes the task much easier!
> - Listen to the example carefully and you will understand that the distractor in this type of question is heard at the start of each utterance.

0 3   classrooms?

_____

[1 mark]

0 4   hall?

_____

[1 mark]

0 5   sports facilities?

_____

[1 mark]

Television and cinema

Listen to your Spanish friends, Pedro and Natalia, talking about films.

What is their opinion of each film type?

Write   **P** for a **positive** opinion.

N for a **negative** opinion.

P+N for a **positive** and **negative** opinion.

Write the correct letter in each box.

> - There are lots of marks available for this type of question, and quite a lot of detail to listen to, so keep a high level of concentration and take brief notes as you listen.
> - Beware of misleading information. For example, in question 6, action films are described as 'never boring' (*nunca son aburridas*).
> - Listen out for expressions that suggest a positive and negative opinion, such as *sin embargo* ('however'), *por otro lado* ('on the other hand') and *aunque* ('although').

0 6   Pedro

action films [   ]   romantic films [   ]

[2 marks]

0 7   Natalia

horror films [   ]   science fiction films [   ]

[2 marks]

AQA GCSE Spanish Foundation Practice Papers © Oxford University Press 2020. Photocopying prohibited.

Helping at home

Your Spanish friends are talking about what chores they do around the house.

Give **two** activities per person.

Write the correct letters in the boxes.

A	Wash the dishes
B	Cook dinner
C	Mow the lawn
D	Babysit
E	Clear the table
F	Vacuum
G	Set the table
H	Clean the bedroom

In this type of question, only listen out for relevant, topic-specific vocabulary: try to ignore any tricky expressions that may cause you to panic and miss the key details that follow. For example, in question 8, many students will not have come across the expression *me toca* ('it's my turn') but this shouldn't be a barrier to giving the correct answer.

0 8 ☐ ☐ **[2 marks]**

0 9 ☐ ☐ **[2 marks]**

1 0 ☐ ☐ **[2 marks]**

1 1 Pascual's revision timetable

You are chatting online to your Spanish friend, Pascual, about exam revision.

Complete each sentence with the correct subject mentioned.

Answer in **English**.

> - Beware of distractors: for example, in question 11, five school subjects are mentioned in total, but two are not relevant to Pascual's revision timetable.
> - You will hear the information in the order of the questions, i.e. the answer to question 11.1 will be near the start and the answer to question 11.3 near the end.
> - Listen out for time markers to help you identify the present, past and then future tenses, for example, Past: *ayer*; Present: *hoy*; Future: *mañana*, as these will help you pinpoint the correct school subject.

1 1 . 1 Today, Pascual is revising . . .

_____

[1 mark]

1 1 . 2 Yesterday, he revised . . .

_____

[1 mark]

1 1 . 3 Tomorrow, he is going to revise . . .

_____

[1 mark]

Protecting the environment

You are listening online to a radio programme. Some Cuban activists are explaining what they do to protect the environment.

Complete the information they give.

Answer in **English**.

Example

This week they have protected <u>abandoned dogs</u> to support <u>animal rights</u>.

> - For this type of question, precision and detail are key. Only include relevant detail in your answers as you can lose marks by adding incorrect information.
> - It is often not enough to recognise and write down one key word that you have understood! For example, in question 13, if you hear '*peces del río local*', make sure you write 'fish from the local river'; you will not be awarded the mark if you simply write 'fish' on its own.

1 2   Next week they will protect _____ to support _____ .

[2 marks]

1 3   Last week they protected _____ to support _____ .

[2 marks]

International food

Listen to Ibrahim and Gloria, your Spanish friends, talking about their favourite countries for food.

For each person, write the correct **letter** in the box for the country they mention.

Write the correct **number** in the box to describe the food from the country they mention.

	Country
A	USA
B	Germany
C	Japan
D	Spain

	Opinion of food
1	Bitter
2	Greasy
3	Salty
4	Spicy

- If you're asked to give a reason for something, listen out for common structures such as *me gusta*, *me encanta*, *odio*, *prefiero X porque es… /son…* Also be alert to negative expressions such as *no*, *nunca*, *nada*.
- Always answer every question and if you're really stuck, make a sensible guess.

1 4   **Ibrahim**

Country   **Opinion**

[2 marks]

1 5   **Gloria**

Country   **Opinion**

[2 marks]

Taking a gap year

You are listening to two students on Spanish radio discussing the value of taking a gap year.

Answer in **English**.

- Read the question carefully to make sure your answers provide the right level of detail. A partial answer, or one that is too vague, will not gain the mark. In question 16, for example, you may hear *otras culturas* ('other cultures'), but in order to gain the mark, you need to expand on that with a suitable verb, such as 'get to know', 'discover', or 'experience'.
- In multiple choice questions in particular, avoid committing to an answer too quickly and always listen carefully to the second playing of the recording, even if you think you have found the correct answer. In question 17, you will hear Elena say '18', 'September' and 'summer', but only one of these answers is correct.

| 1 | 6 |

Why does Elena want to take a gap year abroad?

_____

[1 mark]

| 1 | 7 |

When is she planning to go?

A	In 18 days
B	Next September
C	This summer

[1 mark]

Future plans

You are watching a series online in which one of the characters is discussing her future plans with her father.

Answer in **English**.

> • Always remember to read the question title and setting as these will help you to understand the context of what you are about to hear. If a question begins with 'Why' or you're asked to give a reason for something, the recording will usually include the word *porque* ('because').
> • For this type of question, you should try to write a full sentence; it is not enough to recognise and write down one or two key words that you have understood. For example, in question 18, if you hear *mejor amiga trabaja allí*, make sure you write 'her best friend works there'; you will not be awarded the mark if you simply write 'best friend' on its own.

1 8 Why does the girl want to work in the restaurant?

_____

[1 mark]

1 9 What makes Santiago a good boss to work for?

_____

[1 mark]

Section B   Questions and answers in **Spanish**

Las actividades de tiempo libre

Estás escuchando un programa de radio. Dos chicos hablan sobre su tiempo libre.

¿De qué actividades hablan y cuándo?

Completa la tabla en **español**.

- Always read the question titles carefully so you clearly understand the context of what you are about to hear. There is a lot of information to digest, so try to maintain your concentration and take notes.
- Pay close attention to the example to make sure your answers provide the correct level of detail. In this case, you need to start each free-time phrase with a verb in the infinitive form *(-ar, -er, -ir)*, such as *jugar*.
- Listen out for time markers, for example, Past: *cuando tenía siete años*; Present: *actualmente*; Future: *el año que viene*, as these will help you identify which tense is being used.

---

2 0   Susa

En el pasado	Ahora	En el futuro
		jugar al bádminton

[2 marks]

2 1   Roberto

En el pasado	Ahora	En el futuro
	ver películas	

[2 marks]

2 2   **Una excursión a la ciudad**

Tu amigo Raúl te habla de una excursión a Huelva.

¿Qué va a hacer allí?

A	montar en bicicleta
B	ir a la estación de policía
C	practicar la natación
D	visitar una galería de arte
E	tomar el sol
F	cenar fuera de un restaurante
G	ir al parque zoológico
H	caminar por la costa

- This question requires a lot of inference; you won't hear the vocabulary in A–H at all. Always be on the lookout for synonyms, as they will often lead you to the correct answer: *la estación de policía > la comisaría, caminar > dar un paseo, la costa > la playa*, for example.
- Listen carefully both times and remember, you won't need to get every answer right for a great exam performance.

Escribe la letra correcta en cada casilla.

[4 marks]

END OF QUESTIONS

Answers and mark schemes

AQA GCSE Spanish (9-1)

Foundation Tier Paper 2 Speaking

Time allowed: 7–9 minutes
(+12 minutes' supervised preparation time)

Candidate's material – Role-play and Photo card

Instructions
- During the preparation time you must prepare the Role-play card and Photo card given to you.
- You may make notes during the preparation time on the paper provided by your teacher-examiner. Do not write on the stimulus cards.
- Hand your notes and both stimulus cards to the teacher-examiner before the General Conversation.
- You must ask the teacher-examiner at least one question in the General Conversation.

Information
- The test will last a maximum of 9 minutes and will consist of a Role-play (approximately 2 minutes) and a Photo card (approximately 2 minutes), followed by a General Conversation (3–5 minutes) based on your nominated Theme and the remaining Theme which has not been covered in the Photo card.
- You must **not** use a dictionary at any time during the test. This includes the preparation time.

Teacher Part

Please note: The Practice Paper questions and answers have not been written or approved by AQA.

ROLE-PLAY 1

CANDIDATE'S ROLE

Part 1

Instructions to candidates

Your teacher will play the part of an assistant in a bookshop in Madrid and will speak first.

You should address the assistant as *usted*.

When you see this – **!** – you will have to respond to something you have not prepared.

When you see this – **?** – you will have to ask a question.

Estás hablando con un empleado / una empleada de una librería de Madrid.

- Libro – qué tipo

- **!**

- Tu opinión sobre la librería (**un** detalle)

- **?** Cafetería

- Tu libro favorito y **una** razón

- For the role-play section of your speaking exam, the most important thing is getting the message across clearly, so keep your responses as simple and clear as possible.
- Each response should contain a verb used in the correct form and just enough relevant detail to fulfil the task. For the third bullet point in this task, for example, two marks could be achieved if you say something short and concise such as *Es muy moderna* ('It is very modern').

ROLE-PLAY 2

CANDIDATE'S ROLE

Part 1

Instructions to candidates

Your teacher will play the part of your Spanish friend and will speak first.

You should address your friend as *tú*.

When you see this – **!** – you will have to respond to something you have not prepared.

When you see this – **?** – you will have to ask a question.

Estás hablando con tu amigo español / tu amiga española sobre el instituto.

- Descripción de tu instituto (**un** detalle)

- Tu asignatura favorita y **una** razón

- **!**

- Comida en la cantina (**un** detalle)

- **?** El uniforme

- Foundation-Tier role-plays do not require you to use any past or future tenses.
- You can use the language of the bullet points to help structure your answer, particularly when you are unsure. For example, the second bullet point reads: *tu asignatura favorita y **una** razón* ('your favourite subject and **one** reason'). You could start your response: *Mi asignatura favorita es…*
- Remember to provide a reason for your opinion, preferably using *porque es* + adjective ('because it is…').

ROLE-PLAY 3

CANDIDATE'S ROLE

Part 1

Instructions to candidates

Your teacher will play the part of your Mexican friend and will speak first.

You should address your friend as *tú*.

When you see this – **!** – you will have to respond to something you have not prepared.

When you see this – **?** – you will have to ask a question.

Estás hablando con tu amigo mexicano / tu amiga mexicana sobre llevar una vida sana.

- Tu dieta (**un** detalle)

- **?** Comida mexicana

- Qué haces para estar en forma (**un** detalle)

- **!**

- Drogas – opinión

- Remember you can prepare detailed notes in the preparation time and write down exactly what you are going to say in the role-play tasks (as well as in response to the three prepared questions on the Photo card), so use the 12 minutes wisely.
- The second bullet point requires any clearly understandable question about Mexican food and must include a verb. For example: *¿Cuál es tu opinión sobre la comida mexicana?* For a question task, it is also permissible to give a statement using a verb followed by *¿Y a ti?* For example here, *No me gusta la comida mexicana. ¿Y a ti?* would gain full marks for communication. This way of asking a question will not suit all question tasks, and the question must make sense for the marks to be awarded.

Card A   **Candidate's Photo card**

Part 2

- Look at the photo during the preparation period.

- Make any notes you wish to on an additional piece of paper.

- Your teacher will then ask you questions about the photo and about topics related to **technology in everyday life**.

Your teacher will ask you the following three questions and then **two more questions** which you have not prepared.

- ¿Qué hay en la foto?

- ¿Qué hiciste en Internet el fin de semana pasado?

- ¿Cuáles son los peligros de Internet para los adolescentes?

> - If you do not understand a particular question, you can ask the teacher-examiner in Spanish, at any time during the exam, to repeat it, using *Repite, por favor* or *¿Cómo?* for example.
> - In the Photo card or General Conversation sections, you can also ask the teacher-examiner to re-phrase a question, clarify a particular point or define a particular word: *¿Puede clarificar?* or *¿Qué quiere decir…?* These techniques are known as repair strategies and if you respond to the question successfully after using them, you will be awarded the same mark as if you had understood it originally.

Card B   **Candidate's Photo card**

Part 2

- Look at the photo during the preparation period.

- Make any notes you wish to on an additional piece of paper.

- Your teacher will then ask you questions about the photo and about topics related to **travel and tourism**.

Your teacher will ask you the following three questions and then **two more questions** which you have not prepared.

- ¿Qué hay en la foto?

- ¿Prefieres ir de vacaciones con familia o con amigos? … ¿Por qué?

- ¿Vas a ir de vacaciones a Latinoamérica en el futuro? … ¿Por qué (no)?

- If you feel you have made an error while answering one of the questions from the Photo card, you should quickly and clearly correct yourself in Spanish. You will **not** be penalised for doing so.
- Avoid using English at any point, however, as this will be considered when the teacher-examiner awards the overall mark for the Photo card section.
- Pay close attention to the time frame you need to answer in. The third bullet contains a near future tense *¿Vas a ir…?* ('Are you going to go . . .?)', so a response using the present or near future tense would work well.

Card C   **Candidate's Photo card**

Part 2

- Look at the photo during the preparation period.

- Make any notes you wish to on an additional piece of paper.

- Your teacher will then ask you questions about the photo and about topics related to **life at school/college**.

Your teacher will ask you the following three questions and then **two more questions** which you have not prepared.

- ¿Qué hay en la foto?

- ¿Cuáles son tus asignaturas favoritas? … ¿Por qué?

- ¿Qué actividades escolares hiciste el año pasado?

> - When answering the first question, make sure you describe only what is in the photo, not what there isn't. You may, however, use conjecture if you run out of things to say. For example, you might say something like *Pienso que los estudiantes van a estudiar español por la tarde*.
> - Try to avoid giving opinions on the photo without any justification. For example, *Me encanta la foto* is not a suitable answer on its own, but *Me encanta la foto porque los estudiantes son trabajadores* is fine.

GENERAL CONVERSATION

Part 3

The Photo card is followed by a General Conversation. The first part of the conversation will be on a theme nominated by the candidate and the second part on the other theme not covered by the Photo card. The total time for the General Conversation will be between **three and five minutes** and a similar amount of time should be spent on each theme. Here is a reminder of the three themes:

- Identity and culture

- Local, national, international and global areas of interest

- Current and future study and employment

The following pages show two examples of the general conversation with accompanying commentary on how these conversations would be marked, followed by tasks. You can find two further conversations in the model answers document that accompanies this paper.

Conversation 1: Themes 2 and 1

Y ahora la conversación. Empezamos con el tema dos. ¿Qué haces normalmente en verano?
Normalmente voy a Escocia con mis padres. Paso tres semanas allí.

Háblame de tus vacaciones del año pasado.
Fui a Escocia en avión. Fui a la costa.

¿Dónde te alojaste?
–

¿Estuviste en un hotel?
Sí.

¿Con quién fuiste?
–

¿Qué hiciste allí?
–

¿Qué actividades hiciste?
La natación, el tenis.

¿Qué comiste y bebiste?
La pizza. Me gusta la pizza.

¿Qué planes futuros tienes para tus próximas vacaciones?
–

¿Dónde vives?
Vivo en una ciudad bastante grande con mi familia.

¿Te gusta tu ciudad?
Sí, me gusta mi ciudad.

¿Por qué?
Porque es grande y moderna.

Cambiamos de tema y ahora es el tema uno. ¿Cuál es tu deporte favorito?
Mi deporte favorito es el tenis.

¿Por qué te gusta el tenis?
Me gusta porque es rápido y divertido.

¿Qué actividades vas a hacer este fin de semana?
El tenis y el cine con mis amigos.

¿Qué película vas a ver?
–

¿Prefieres ir al cine o ver la televisión?
Siempre el cine. Es muy entretenido.

Pero el cine es caro, ¿no?
Sí, es caro.

¿Qué programas te gustan en la tele?
No me gusta la tele.

¿Te gusta leer?
Sí, me gusta leer.

Háblame de algo que hayas leído recientemente.
–

¿Qué vas a leer próximamente?
–

¿Qué aplicaciones usas?
Uso Instagram y Spotify. Me gusta escuchar música.

¿Qué es lo bueno y lo malo de las redes sociales?
–

¿Tienes alguna pregunta para mí?
–

Marks and commentary

	Communication	Range and accuracy of language	Pronunciation and intonation	Spontaneity and fluency	Total
Marks	5/10	5/10	3/5	2/5	15/30

This conversation receives 5 marks for Communication. A few responses are detailed but unfortunately, many questions are unanswered or the response is repeating what the teacher-examiner has said. A further mark is lost for not asking a question.

5 marks are awarded for Range and accuracy of language. A past-tense verb is used on only one occasion and the language is often basic and repetitive.

Pronunciation and intonation are assumed to be of a reasonable standard, so gain 3 marks.

For Spontaneity and fluency, 2 marks are given. Many questions do not receive an answer and other responses are basic and hesitant. There is no evidence of any flow to the conversation.

1. In the conversation the expression *me gusta* is used five times. What other expressions could be used instead?

2. Answer the questions for yourself about a past holiday (second to eighth question). Check that you have used a suitable past tense and include as much detail as possible.

Conversation 2: Themes 2 and 1

Y ahora la conversación. Empezamos con el tema dos. ¿Qué haces normalmente en verano?
Normalmente voy a Escocia con mis padres. Me alojo en un camping en el norte. Llueve mucho pero el camping es muy cómodo y lo paso bien allí.

Háblame de tus vacaciones del año pasado.
El pasado abril fui a Mallorca en avión. Me alojé en un hotel de cerca de la playa.

¿Qué hiciste en Mallorca?
Tomé el sol y nadé en el mar. Además, fui a una catedral que se llama La Seu.

¿Qué tal la gastronomía del lugar?
Es deliciosa. Comí paella todos los días.

¿Hablaste mucho español en Mallorca?
Sí, hablé español muchas veces.

¿Qué planes futuros tienes para tus próximas vacaciones?
Voy a ir a México porque es un país fascinante.

¿Qué harás allí?
Voy a visitar muchos monumentos como Tulum.

¿Dónde vives?
Vivo en una ciudad bastante grande con mi familia. Y tú, ¿dónde vives?

Vivo en un pueblo pequeño. ¿Te gusta tu ciudad?
Sí, me gusta mi ciudad. Es grande y moderna. Lo bueno es que hay mucho que hacer.

Cambiamos de tema y ahora es el tema uno. ¿Cuál es tu deporte favorito?
Mi deporte favorito es el tenis. Me gusta Rafa Nadal. No juego a muchos deportes de equipo porque no tengo tiempo.

¿Qué actividades vas a hacer este fin de semana?
Este fin de semana voy a ir al cine con mis amigos. Vamos a ver una película de acción.

¿Prefieres ver las películas en el cine o en casa?
Prefiero ir al cine porque la pantalla es enorme y me gusta salir con mis amigos.

¿Qué programas te gustan en la tele?
Veo un concurso tres veces a la semana. No veo muchas series porque no tengo tiempo.

¿Te gustan las redes sociales?
Me mola Twitter porque hay muchas opiniones diferentes. No uso ni Instagram ni Facebook.

¿Qué es lo malo de las redes sociales?
Hay problemas de acoso en las redes sociales. Es muy triste.

Marks and commentary

	Communication	Range and accuracy of language	Pronunciation and intonation	Spontaneity and fluency	Total
Marks	10/10	10/10	5/5	5/5	30/30

This conversation has been given 10 marks for Communication. In contrast to the first response, these answers are generally very detailed, with original content and opinions, some of which are explained, such as *Me mola Twitter porque hay muchas opiniones diferentes.*

10 marks are awarded for Range and accuracy of language. Three time frames are successfully used and there are several complex structures and examples of ambitious vocabulary, for example, *Lo bueno es que hay mucho que hacer* and *hay problemas de acoso* that would be suitable for success even at Higher Tier.

Given the quality of the content and language, pronunciation and intonation are assumed to be very good, so gain 5 marks.

For Spontaneity and fluency, 5 marks are given. The conversation appears to flow naturally and without hesitation.

1. In the conversation find examples of:

   • any Spanish cultural references

   • opinions that are explained.

2. Re-read the two answers to the question *¿Qué haces normalmente en verano?* Compare the answer of model answer 1 with that of model answer 2. Explain why the second answer is better, then write your own answer to the question, using model answer 2 as guidance.

Model answers and mark schemes

AQA GCSE Spanish Foundation Practice Papers © Oxford University Press 2020. Photocopying prohibited.

Foundation Tier Paper 3 Reading

Time allowed: 45 minutes

Instructions
- Answer **all** questions.
- Answer the questions in the spaces provided.
- In **Section A**, answer the questions in **English**. In **Section B**, answer the questions in **Spanish**. In **Section C**, translate the passage into **English**.
- Cross through any work you do not want to be marked.

Information
- The marks for the questions are shown in brackets.
- The maximum mark for this paper is 60.
- You must **not** use a dictionary.

Please note: The Practice Paper questions and answers have not been written or approved by AQA.

Section A Questions and answers in **English**

| 0 | 1 | **An invitation**

Your Mexican friend, Hugo, sends you a birthday invitation.

> El sábado que viene mi hermanastra Paula va a celebrar su fiesta de quinceañera y hemos organizado una fiesta maravillosa.
>
> ¿Puedes acompañarnos?
>
> Estaremos en el restaurante Los Molinos desde las nueve hasta entrada la madrugada.

Answer the questions in **English**.

Whenever you think you may not know a particular word, educated guesses can be highly effective. For example, in 1.1, *hermanastra* looks like 'sister' and *quinceañera* contains the word 'fifteen'. Even words that appear impossible to understand will often contain clues within them that can help lead you to the correct answer!

| 0 | 1 | . | 1 | What relation is Paula to Hugo?

_____

[1 mark]

| 0 | 1 | . | 2 | How old is Paula going to be?

_____

[1 mark]

| 0 | 1 | . | 3 | When will the party finish?

Write the correct letter in the box.

A	Midnight
B	Early morning
C	9pm

[ ] **[1 mark]**

0 2 **Stress in school**

You read these young people's opinions about stress in their school lives on an online forum in Spain.

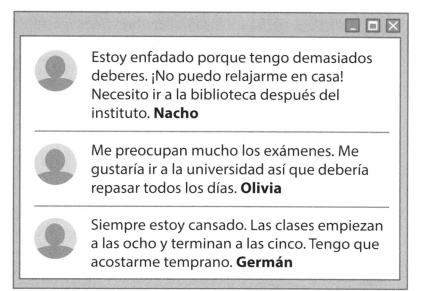

> Estoy enfadado porque tengo demasiados deberes. ¡No puedo relajarme en casa! Necesito ir a la biblioteca despúes del instituto. **Nacho**
>
> Me preocupan mucho los exámenes. Me gustaría ir a la universidad así que debería repasar todos los días. **Olivia**
>
> Siempre estoy cansado. Las clases empiezan a las ocho y terminan a las cinco. Tengo que acostarme temprano. **Germán**

If an example is provided, read it carefully, as it may give you key information that can help you answer the questions that follow. The example answer in 2.1, 'Go to the library after school', suggests that when answering the question 'what does he/she need to do?' in 2.2 and 2.3, you will need to provide two pieces of information.

For each student, complete the table in **English**.

0 2 . 1

How does Nacho feel?	What does he need to do?
	Go to the library after school

[1 mark]

0 2 . 2

How does Olivia feel?	What does she need to do?

[2 marks]

0 2 . 3

How does Germán feel?	What does he need to do?
Tired	

[1 mark]

| 0 | 3 |

La más bella niña, a poem by Luis de Góngora

Read the opening lines of the poem and answer the questions that follow.

La más bella niña
De nuestro lugar,
Hoy viuda y sola
Y ayer por casar,
Viendo que sus ojos
A la guerra van,
A su madre dice,
Que escucha su mal:
Dejadme llorar
Orillas del mar.

Write the correct letter in each box.

- Literary texts are often presented differently to the other questions in your paper. They may be in the form of a dialogue, a set of stage directions, or as a poem. They are also likely to contain some unfamiliar vocabulary. Fortunately, the questions you answer usually follow a familiar format, so use your usual exam techniques.
- If you have to take a guess, however, avoid distractors – the most obvious answer is rarely the right one! For example, in 3.2, you might link *bella* to getting married or engaged, but fail to spot that the girl is alone (*sola*) today (*hoy*), whereas she was to be married (*por casar*) yesterday (*ayer*).

| 0 | 3 |.| 1 | The girl is…

A	kind.
B	beautiful.
C	happy.

[1 mark]

0 3 . 2 From today, the girl is…

A	widowed.
B	married.
C	engaged.

[1 mark]

0 3 . 3 She wants her mother to…

A	talk to her.
B	listen to her.
C	leave her alone.

[1 mark]

0 3 . 4 At the end, she would like to…

A	play.
B	think.
C	cry.

[1 mark]

| 0 | 4 | **Catalina de Santiago, a pioneering scientist**

You are reading this article in a Spanish magazine about Catalina's accomplishments.

Catalina es una de las científicas más prominentes de España. Era una niña imaginativa, y tuvo una infancia feliz viviendo con sus padres cariñosos en un lugar idílico.

Empezó a investigar hace veinte años en su ciudad natal, Vigo. Cuando tenía catorce años ganó su primer premio en una competición científica de su comunidad autónoma, y después, a los dieciséis años, ganó la competición nacional.

En la Universidad Autónoma de Madrid, Catalina y sus compañeros de laboratorio acaban de descubrir importantes mejoras para las enfermedades de la vista.

Write the correct letter in each box.

In multiple-choice questions, many or all of the answers seem possible. This is deliberate to really test your comprehension skills. Look very carefully at the relevant part of the text and read it over and over until you are sure of the meaning, then try to rule out the other options. For example, in 4.1, you might correctly spot the adjectives 'loving' (*cariñosos*) and 'idyllic' (*idílico*) in the text, but in order to answer the question, you need to identify the adjective used to describe the noun 'childhood' (*infancia*).

| 0 | 4 | . | 1 | What was Catalina's childhood like?

A	Loving
B	Idyllic
C	Happy

[1 mark]

| 0 | 4 | . | 2 | How old was Catalina when she won a regional science competition?

A	14
B	16
C	20

[1 mark]

0 4 . 3 Catalina and her colleagues have made important discoveries in which area?

A	Skin conditions
B	Respiratory illnesses
C	Eye diseases

[1 mark]

| 0 | 5 |

Vocational courses

While browsing a Spanish college website you read about the courses they offer.

A	Business Management
B	Interior Design
C	Piano Level 2
D	Food Technology
E	Travel and Tourism
F	Hairdressing

What courses can you study?

Write the correct letter in each box.

- You will probably know most of the vocabulary required to gain full marks on question 5, but you need care and attention to do so. Look for small clues, especially cognates such as *clásica* (classical), *cliente* (customer), *vacacional* (holiday), or *promocionar* (promote) that will help you find the correct answer.
- Read statements 5.1–5.4 and translate any words you know into English. Re-read the statements and then try to translate those words you didn't work out the first time, looking for clues from context.

| 0 | 5 | . | 1 |

Aprender a tocar más rápidamente y con fluidez, piezas clásicas y modernas.

[1 mark]

| 0 | 5 | . | 2 |

Aprender a atender al cliente, ofrecer actividades extra y completar un viaje vacacional.

[1 mark]

| 0 | 5 | . | 3 |

Aprender qué alimentos combinan mejor para llevar una vida sana.

[1 mark]

| 0 | 5 | . | 4 |

Aprender a promocionar un negocio y vender en línea.

[1 mark]

0 6 **Esteban's project**

You are reading this article on a Spanish website about how Esteban redeveloped an entire village.

> Cuando Esteban era pequeño y vivía con sus padres en un pequeño apartamento en el centro de Sevilla, a veces lloraba porque no tenía espacio para jugar.
>
> Sin embargo, a los veinticinco años vio una oferta en Internet para comprar una aldea abandonada por cien euros . . . ¡y decidió hacerlo!
>
> Trece años después, Esteban ha transformado la aldea. El antiguo instituto de la aldea ya es la casa de sus sueños. Además, todos sus familiares viven en las casas renovadas al lado. ¡Qué final tan feliz!

- Remember that the answers are always in the order of the reading texts, i.e. the answer to question 6.1 will be near the start and the answer to question 6.4 near the end.
- Answer every question and if in doubt, guess something. You may not know that *lloraba* means 'he used to cry', but you may know words such as *un apartamento pequeño, a veces, espacio* and *jugar*. By piecing these clues together, you can reach the answer to 6.1.

Answer the questions in **English**.

0 6 . 1 Why did Esteban sometimes cry when he was little?

_____

[1 mark]

0 6 . 2 How much did he pay for the village?

_____

[1 mark]

0 6 . 3 What did Esteban turn the local school into?

_____

[1 mark]

0 6 . 4 Where do Esteban's family live?

_____

[1 mark]

| 0 | 7 |

Free-time activities

You read this interview in a Chilean magazine featuring Lorena Márquez, a reality TV star.

> – **Lorena, ¿qué sueles hacer en tu tiempo libre?**
> – Las actividades acuáticas me interesan mucho. Actualmente, voy a una piscina cubierta local para nadar. Pronto me uniré al club de polo acuático que hay allí también.
>
> – **¿Practicas otros deportes acuáticos en este momento?**
> – No. Hace cinco años lo que me fascinaba era el submarinismo, pero hoy en día prefiero caminar por la montaña.
>
> – **Lorena, ¿estás en contra de la pesca?**
> – Por supuesto. De pequeña pasaba tranquila muchas tardes a orillas del río Cisnes pescando con mi padre, pero la falta de humanidad de los pescadores ahora me parece insoportable.

At which point in time of Lorena's life do the following water sports apply?

Write   **P** for something that happened in the **past**.

N for something that is happening **now**.

F for something that is going to happen in the **future**.

Write the correct letter in each box.

To answer these questions correctly, first, identify any time phrases. Then, separate any tenses into two categories. Here is a reminder of their formation:
- Present, preterite and imperfect tenses: remove the last two letters of the infinitive and add the correct endings.
- Future tense and conditional: add the correct endings to the infinitive.

| 0 7 . 1 | Swimming | | **[1 mark]** |

| 0 7 . 2 | Water polo | | **[1 mark]** |

| 0 7 . 3 | Scuba diving | | **[1 mark]** |

| 0 7 . 4 | Fishing | | **[1 mark]** |

0 8   **Pets in Spain**

You read this article about pets in a Spanish magazine.

España, el país amante de las mascotas

Los amantes de las mascotas son más numerosos en España ahora que hace diez años. La mayoría de los 13 millones de mascotas registradas no vive en el campo, sino en las ciudades. Un estudio reciente afirma que la soledad de la vida ciudadana hoy en día es la causa principal de este aumento.

En Gijón, las mascotas ya están integradas en la vida cotidiana y hay cada vez más zonas verdes donde puedes pasear con el perro suelto. Lorenzo, un gijonés que vive con su perro en un piso de un dormitorio, dice que no le importa el alto coste mensual de mantener su perro porque no podría vivir sin él. Sin embargo, no siempre fue así. Cuando Lorenzo era pequeño, el dueño del apartamento de la familia no le permitía tener animales en casa.

Which **three** statements are true?

Write the correct letters in the boxes.

- When reading a news item or article, read the title carefully as it can set the tone of the information that follows. For example, the title declares that Spain is a country that loves pets and some of statements A–F echo this sentiment.
- Read statements A–F carefully and highlight any key words before checking the text to see if there is a match. In paragraph 2, for example, the phrase *el alto coste* is preceded by *no le importa*, which should lead you to the correct answer E.

A	10 years ago there were fewer pet lovers in Spain.
B	Most pet owners in Spain live in the countryside.
C	Loneliness is now the main reason for pet ownership in cities.
D	In Gijón, dogs must be on leads at all times.
E	Lorenzo is not worried about the high cost of dog ownership.
F	Lorenzo's family did not allow him to have a pet when he was little.

[ ] [ ] [ ]

[3 marks]

0 9   **Sports for everyone**

You read an article in a Colombian newspaper about sports.

> **Los deportes no tienen límites**
>
> La semana que viene la ciudad de Bogotá inaugura sus Campeonatos de Deportes Inclusivos.
>
> En estos campeonatos hay atletismo, baloncesto, tenis y natación.
>
> En las cuatro categorías no hay separación por capacidades. Las personas ciegas, sordas o con problemas de movilidad pueden participar con el resto de deportistas, sin sentirse inferiores.

Decide if the following statements are true (**T**), false (**F**) or not mentioned (**NM**) in the text.

Write   **T** if the statement is **true**.

    F if the statement is **false**.

    NM if the statement is **not mentioned** in the text.

Write the correct letter(s) in each box.

- The 'NM' ('Not Mentioned') answers often cause confusion. If there is not enough evidence to decide whether a statement is true or false, the answer should be 'NM'. Even if a statement might be true, such as 9.4 for example, if it isn't mentioned in the text, it must be 'NM'.
- If you need to change an answer, cross out the incorrect letter and write the new one(s) clearly.

0 9 . 1   The Inclusive Sports Championships took place last week in Bogotá.

[1 mark]

0 9 . 2   Swimming is the most popular sport at the Championships.

[1 mark]

0 9 . 3   Athletes are of mixed ability in all of the events.

[1 mark]

0 9 . 4   The number of athletes participating this year has fallen.

[1 mark]

Section B   Questions and answers in **Spanish**

| 1 | 0 | | **Los parques naturales españoles** |

Ves esta página en una revista sobre los parques naturales de España.

A	En Cabañeros, hay más de veinte kilómetros de caminos a través del campo para explorar la naturaleza.
B	En Las Tablas de Daimiel, puedes observar a los patos y otros pájaros típicos del centro del país.
C	En Los Picos de Europa hace muchísimo frío en invierno y hay nieve. Necesitarás un abrigo.
D	¡Doñana es tan diverso! Aquí hay playas inmensas con arena suave.
E	Garajonay te sorprenderá por sus praderas verdes. ¡Tienes que verlas desde un helicóptero!
F	El parque del Teide es el único en España que tiene un volcán . . . no es peligroso, pero está activo.

¿Cuál es el lugar ideal para estas personas?

Escribe la letra correcta en cada casilla.

> • For this type of reading activity, use a process of elimination by first identifying key words or phrases in statements 10.1–10.4 to help lead you to the right answer.
> • Don't guess too soon: in 10.2, you might consider *las temperaturas bajas* (low temperatures) important, and after scanning the headings A–F, earmark C, as it mentions multiple key words: *frío, nieve* and *abrigo* which correspond.
> • Always be on the lookout for synonyms, as they will often lead you to the correct answer; *la costa > la playa*, for example.

| 1 | 0 | . | 1 | Me gustan las vistas desde el aire. | | **[1 mark]** |

| 1 | 0 | . | 2 | No me importan las temperaturas bajas. | | **[1 mark]** |

| 1 | 0 | . | 3 | Me entusiasma observar aves. | | **[1 mark]** |

| 1 | 0 | . | 4 | Quiero tomar el sol en la costa. | | **[1 mark]** |

1 1 **Una obra de teatro**

Lees este comentario sobre una obra de teatro.

> *Aventuras en La Mancha* es una obra de teatro musical muy original que cuenta cómo los protagonistas, Mercedes y Andrés, dos estudiantes de dieciséis años, se conocieron. La historia es sencilla y graciosa, y tiene bailes increíbles.

¿Cómo se describe la obra?

Escribe las letras en las casillas.

> - This sort of question requires an awareness of synonyms and good exam technique. Firstly, find and highlight the adjectives in the text, then try to match each of them to the adjectives in the list A–F.
> - Try to avoid being distracted by any language that is not needed to complete the task successfully.
> - If in doubt, do not leave any boxes blank, especially in questions like these where you have to write a letter: have a guess!

A	lenta
B	cómica
C	histórica
D	compleja
E	simple
F	única

☐ ☐ ☐

[3 marks]

1 2 **Opiniones sobre la Tomatina de Buñol**

¿Cuál es la opinión de cada persona sobre la Tomatina de Buñol?

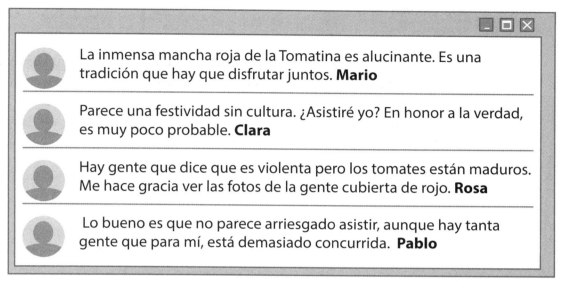

La inmensa mancha roja de la Tomatina es alucinante. Es una tradición que hay que disfrutar juntos. **Mario**

Parece una festividad sin cultura. ¿Asistiré yo? En honor a la verdad, es muy poco probable. **Clara**

Hay gente que dice que es violenta pero los tomates están maduros. Me hace gracia ver las fotos de la gente cubierta de rojo. **Rosa**

Lo bueno es que no parece arriesgado asistir, aunque hay tanta gente que para mí, está demasiado concurrida. **Pablo**

Escribe   **P** si la opinión es **positiva**.

          N si la opinión es **negativa**.

          P+N si la opinión es **positiva** y **negativa**.

Escribe la(s) letra(s) correcta(s) en cada casilla.

- Highlight any adjectives, verbs or phrases that might be used to express a positive or negative opinion such as *disfrutar* (to enjoy), *poco probable* (not very probable) and *lo bueno* (the good thing).
- Be careful: statements that seem positive or negative at the start, such as Pablo's for example, often contain conjunctions of contrast such as *aunque* (although), *pero* (but), *sin embargo* (however), *mientras* (while), followed later on with a counter opinion, in which case the answer is usually P+N.

1 2 . 1   Mario   **[1 mark]**

1 2 . 2   Clara   **[1 mark]**

1 2 . 3   Rosa   **[1 mark]**

1 2 . 4   Pablo   **[1 mark]**

1 3   **El transporte**

Ves en una revista ecuatoriana esta página de opiniones sobre los medios de transporte urbanos.

Personalmente me chifla vivir en la ciudad capital, pero raras veces quiero montar en taxis porque cuestan mucho dinero. Los autocares urbanos son muy económicos, aunque mi padre prefiere viajar en metro porque en su opinión, es más seguro. **Lucrecia**	Cuando me levanto temprano para ir al instituto no es posible ir en bicicleta debido a la oscuridad. Mi madre tiene un coche pequeño y nos lleva a mi hermana y a mí. A mis amigos les gusta ir juntos en autobús. **Adrián**

Completa las frases en **español**.

Ejemplo   A Lucrecia le gusta…

<u>vivir en la ciudad capital.</u>

> - Sentence-completion questions involve a similar technique to questions that require an answer in Spanish.
> - Pay close attention to the example, if one is provided, so that you know how to answer. In this case, a phrase starting with an infinitive verb (ending in *-ar, -er* or *-ir*) is required for each answer.
> - Look for an expression in the text with roughly the same meaning as the verb at the end of each unfinished statement in 13.1–13.4. In the example, *le gusta…* ('she likes' in the statement) = *me chifla* ('I love' in the text); the answer phrase comes directly after it.

1 3 . 1   Lucrecia casi nunca quiere…

_____

[1 mark]

1 3 . 2   El padre de Lucrecia recomienda…

_____

[1 mark]

1 3 . 3   Para ir al instituto, Adrián no puede…

_____

[1 mark]

1 3 . 4   A los compañeros de Adrián les gusta…

_____

[1 mark]

1 4   **Los datos de los adolescentes de hoy**

Lees este artículo sobre los adolescentes españoles.

> De los 100 adolescentes encuestados:
>
> el 78% ve las series en servicios bajo demanda en línea.
> el 70% se preocupa por su apariencia.
> el 33% no tiene la intención de ir a la universidad.
> el 27% ha sufrido acoso escolar.
> el 22% tiene problemas de salud mental.
> el 8% no come carne.

¿Qué porcentaje de los adolescentes españoles corresponde a cada frase?

Escribe el porcentaje correcto en cada casilla.

Ejemplo   Es vegetariano.   8

> Make sure you read the example carefully and look for cognates or near-cognates that can help you find the correct answer, for example, *psicológico* (psychological) > *mental*, *físico* (physical) > *apariencia* (appearance).

1 4 . 1   Sufre trastornos psicológicos.   **[1 mark]**

1 4 . 2   Se interesa por su aspecto físico.   **[1 mark]**

1 4 . 3   Ha sido intimidado en el instituto.   **[1 mark]**

Section C   Translation into **English**

1 5   Your Spanish exchange partner sends you this message.

Translate it into **English** for a friend.

> • You need to be as precise as possible in translation activities, especially with any tenses: when translating *iré al cine*, for example, you must use the future tense in English 'I will go to the cinema', as the present tense 'I go/I am going' won't gain any marks.
> • When you have finished, read over your translation to check it reads well and use your common sense to correct any odd turns of phrase – for example, in English we say 'at home', not 'in home'. Likewise, 'war films' is more natural in English than 'films of war'.

> No me interesan las películas de guerra porque son una pérdida de tiempo. Mañana, iré al cine con mi primo. Prefiero ver las series en casa porque son más entretenidas. ¡El mes pasado compré una televisión con una pantalla enorme!

[9 marks]

_____

_____

_____

_____

_____

_____

_____

END OF QUESTIONS

Answers and mark schemes

Foundation Tier Paper 4 Writing

Time allowed: 1 hour

Instructions

- You must answer **four** questions.
- You must answer Question 1, Question 2 and Question 3.
- You must answer **either** Question 4.1 **or** Question 4.2. Do not answer **both** of these questions.
- Answer all questions in **Spanish**.
- Answer the questions in the spaces provided.
- Cross through any work you do not want to be marked.

Information

- The marks for the questions are shown in brackets.
- The maximum mark for this paper is 50.
- You must **not** use a dictionary during this test.
- In order to score the highest marks for Question 4.1/Question 4.2, you must write something about each bullet point. You must use a variety of vocabulary and structures and include your opinions.

Please note: The Practice Paper questions and answers have not been written or approved by AQA.

Answer the questions in the spaces provided.

| 0 | 1 | Decides colgar esta foto en Instagram para tus amigos mexicanos.

Escribe **cuatro** frases en **español** que describan la foto.

> - For question 1, you should avoid writing overly ambitious sentences or you run the risk of making a serious error that affects communication.
> - Always include a verb but keep sentences short and simple to make sure you communicate a clear message.
> - It is acceptable to repeat the same grammatical structure in more than one sentence, so you could simply use the verb *hay* with a different object from the photo for each of the four sentences to gain full marks.

| 0 | 1 |.| 1 |

_____

[2 marks]

| 0 | 1 |.| 2 |

_____

[2 marks]

| 0 | 1 |.| 3 |

_____

[2 marks]

| 0 | 1 |.| 4 |

_____

[2 marks]

0	2

Tu amiga colombiana, Amelia, te ha preguntado sobre tu instituto.

Escríbele un email.

Menciona:

- instalaciones

- horario

- reglas

- uniforme

Escribe aproximadamente **40** palabras en **español**.

[16 marks]

- You need to cover all four bullet points in your answer to get the top marks for content, but there is no need for equal coverage of each one. When tackling the third bullet point, for instance, you might feel you don't know a lot of vocabulary relating to 'rules' (*reglas*), in which case you can give your opinion of them instead.
- Try to vary your language by using a variety of verbs such as *me encanta(n), me chifla(n)*, as well as alternative adjectives such as *divertido* or *emocionante*.
- Make sure you check that your verb endings and adjectival agreements are correct.

0 3   Translate the following sentences into **Spanish**.

> • Each sentence is broken down into two or three parts, each of which receives a tick if translated correctly. These ticks are then added up and converted into an overall mark. As a general rule, use of the wrong person or tense of a verb will not receive a tick, so your revision for this part of the writing exam should involve practising common verbs in all persons in the present, preterite and near future tenses.
> • Practise translations as much as possible. After a while, you will find that the same high-frequency words, phrases and even general vocabulary come up regularly, such as days of the week and time phrases.

My parents are very generous.

_____

I listen to music with my brother.

_____

I eat a chocolate ice-cream.

_____

There are many interesting monuments in my town.

_____

Next year I want to live on the coast.

_____

[10 marks]

Answer **either** Question 4.1 **or** Question 4.2.
You must **not** answer **both** of these questions.

EITHER Question 4.1

| 0 | 4 | . | 1 | Ves una página web con el título, 'Cómo cuidar de tu barrio'.

Decides escribir sobre tu barrio.

Menciona:

- tus sitios favoritos en tu barrio

- qué hiciste en tu barrio la semana pasada

- qué se debe hacer para cuidar bien de tu barrio

- dónde te gustaría vivir en el futuro.

Escribe aproximadamente **90** palabras en **español**.
Responde a todos los aspectos de la pregunta.

[16 marks]

> - To give your response a clear structure, try to answer the bullets in order and tick them off on the exam paper as you do so.
> - Identify which bullet points target the different time frames and check that your tenses are accurate. For example, the second bullet contains the preterite *hiciste*, so you need to refer to the past in your answer.
> - Look out for bullet points that offer language that you can use in your answer. For example, the third bullet point *qué se debe hacer para cuidar bien de tu barrio* gives you an ideal start to a sentence: *Para cuidar bien de mi barrio…*

OR Question 4.2

| 0 | 4 | . | 2 | Tu amiga española, Sara, te pregunta sobre las Navidades en tu país.

Escríbele un email.

Menciona:

- qué hiciste el día de Navidad el año pasado

- tu opinión sobre las Navidades

- qué fiestas te gustan más

- qué fiesta española o latinoamericana te gustaría ver en persona.

Escribe aproximadamente **90** palabras en **español**.
Responde a todos los aspectos de la pregunta.

[16 marks]

> - When revising for your writing exam, learn a handful of impressive expressions and opinions.
> - Opinions are needed in the second and third bullets and you will gain higher marks if you include a variety of verbs and vocabulary in your answer.
> - Think about which bullet points require the past tense (1) and which require the future (4).

_____

_____

_____

_____

_____

_____

_____

_____

_____

_____

_____

_____

_____

_____

_____

_____

_____

END OF QUESTIONS

Model answers and mark schemes

AQA GCSE Spanish (9-1)

F

Foundation Tier Paper 1 Listening

Time allowed: 35 minutes
(including 5 minutes' reading time before the test)

You will need no other materials.
The pauses are pre-recorded for this test.

Information
- The marks for the questions are shown in brackets. The maximum mark for this paper is 40.
- You must **not** use a dictionary.

Advice
This is what you should do for each item.
- After the question number is announced, there will be a pause to allow you to read the instructions and questions.
- Listen carefully to the recording and read the questions again.
- Listen to the recording again, and then answer the questions.
- When the next question is about to start you will hear a bleep.
- You may write at any time during the test.
- In **Section A**, answer the questions in **English**. In **Section B**, answer the questions in **Spanish**.
- You must answer all the questions in the spaces provided. Do not write on blank pages.
- Write neatly and put down all the information you are asked to give.
- **You must not ask questions or interrupt during the test.**
- You have five minutes to read through the question paper. You may make notes during this time. You may turn to the questions now.
- **The test starts now.**

Listen to the audio

Please note: The Practice Paper questions and answers have not been written or approved by AQA.

Section A   Questions and answers in **English**

Health and well-being

While in Tenerife, you listen to a radio programme in which people discuss their lifestyle problems.

A	Loneliness
B	High sugar intake
C	Lack of sleep
D	Internet addiction
E	Workplace stress
F	Lack of exercise
G	Money worries
H	Drug abuse

Give **two** problems per person.

Write the correct letters in the boxes.

> In multiple-choice questions, use some of your preparation time to anticipate and note down words you might hear, using the headings (here A–H) as a guide. So, for example, listen carefully for words such as 'stress/stressful' (*el estrés/estresante*), 'money' (*dinero*), 'to sleep' (*dormir*) or 'drugs' (*las drogas*), and rule out the most unlikely answer(s) as soon as possible.

| 0 | 1 | [2 marks]

| 0 | 2 | [2 marks]

| 0 | 3 | [2 marks]

Family birthdays

While in Barcelona, your Spanish friends discuss upcoming birthday celebrations.

Which **two** things does each person mention?

Write the correct letters in the boxes.

0	4

A	How old he is going to be
B	The location of the party
C	Sending invitations
D	His parents' concerns

☐ ☐

[2 marks]

0	5

A	The date of her birthday
B	The presents she will receive
C	The type of birthday cake she wants
D	Her mum's personality

☐ ☐

[2 marks]

| 0 | 6 | **Social issues**

You are watching a Spanish television debate in which people are discussing social issues that concern them.

For each speaker, choose their area of concern.

Write the correct letter in each box.

A	Health care
B	Youth unemployment rate
C	Knife crime
D	The housing market
E	Family conflict

Answer all parts of the question.

> - It is unlikely that the key words in the statements A–E will be the same as those you hear in the audio! Try to think of Spanish words associated with some of these headings which you can listen out for: 'health' (*la salud*), 'unemployment' (*el paro*), 'jobs' (*los empleos*), 'housing' (*la vivienda*), 'knife' (*el cuchillo*), for example.
> - You will probably hear words that seem to refer to many possible answers. Try to get a feeling for the topic being discussed and to avoid being thrown off course by single words.

| 6 | . | 1 | Diana | | **[1 mark]** |

| 6 | . | 2 | Gerardo | | **[1 mark]** |

| 6 | . | 3 | Pamela | | **[1 mark]** |

Films

Some Mexican friends are talking about the types of film they like and why.

Type of film

A	Horror
B	Comedy
C	War
D	Animation

Reason

1	Funny
2	Exciting
3	Scary
4	Emotional

For each person, write the correct **letter** in the box for the type of film they mention.

Write the correct **number** in the box for the reason they give.

Before you sit your exams, make sure you have access to plenty of listening tasks such as these that try to trick you, and perfect your technique of spotting distractors and 'false friends' (i.e. Spanish words that resemble English words, but have a different meaning). If you don't pay close attention, you may be drawn to the wrong answer!

| 0 | 7 | Marialen

Film   **Reason**

[2 marks]

| 0 | 8 | Nico

Film   **Reason**

[2 marks]

Activities at home

Your Spanish friend, Luis, is telling you about how he spends his time at home.

Answer in **English**.

What activity does he do…

Example   in the living room? <u>Listens to music</u>

| 0 | 9 | in his bedroom?

_____

[1 mark]

| 1 | 0 | in the kitchen?

_____

[1 mark]

| 1 | 1 | in the dining room?

_____

[1 mark]

Opinions about a new school in Tenerife

Listen to your Spanish friends, Natalia and Luis, talking about their new school building.

What are their opinions on the new school's facilities?

Write   **P** if the opinion is **positive**.

N if the opinion is **negative**.

P+N if the opinion is **positive** and **negative**.

Write the correct letter in each box.

| 1 | 2 | **Natalia**

The library [   ] and the laboratories [   ]   [2 marks]

| 1 | 3 | **Luis**

The swimming pool [   ] and the canteen [   ]   [2 marks]

A visit to Madrid

While on holiday in Madrid you talk to a tourist guide about what to see.

Complete each recommendation.

Answer in **English**.

Example

On Friday you could go to the <u>theatre</u> because there will be a <u>classical music concert</u>.

> If an example is provided, read it carefully, as it may give you key information that can help you answer the questions that follow. The example shows that you need to write a place in town (i.e. 'theatre') for the first mark and an event that takes place there (i.e. 'classical music concert') for the second mark. You would not gain a mark for simply stating 'concert'. For this type of question, precision and detail are key. Only include relevant detail in your answers as you can lose marks by adding incorrect information.

1 4   On Tuesday you could go to the _____ because there

will be a _____.   **[2 marks]**

1 5   On Sunday you could go to the _____ because there

will be a _____.   **[2 marks]**

Family relationships

You are watching an interview on Argentinian TV in which a family psychologist describes his new series.

Answer the questions in **English**.

> Read the question carefully to make sure your answers provide the right level of detail. A partial answer, or one that is too vague, will not gain the mark. Always listen carefully to the second playing of the recording even if you think you have found the correct answer. Above all, make sure you try to answer all questions.

1 6   What problem will the first programme discuss?

_____

[1 mark]

1 7   Who will be the guest in the second programme?

_____

[1 mark]

1 8   **A gap year**

Your friend from El Salvador, Elías, is talking to his teacher about his plans for after the exams.

You listen to the conversation.

Answer **both** parts of the question in **English**.

1 8 . 1   What does Elías intend to do on his gap year?

_____

_____

[1 mark]

1 8 . 2   What is his teacher's recommendation?

_____

_____

[1 mark]

Section B   Questions and answers in **Spanish**

El tiempo libre

Estás con tus dos amigos, Valeria y Santi. Están hablando sobre su tiempo libre.

¿De qué hablan y cuándo?

Completa la tabla en **español**.

> - For this type of question, make sure you write your answer in Spanish (as shown in the example). If you have understood the material well, it is tempting to translate it into English, but you won't get any marks for doing so.
> - In this case, the infinitive form of the verb (i.e. *leer* or *seguir*) is required at the start of each answer. Realising this makes the task much easier!

1 9   **Valeria**

En el pasado	Ahora	En el futuro
leer novelas de aventuras		

[2 marks]

2 0   **Santi**

En el pasado	Ahora	En el futuro
	seguir la moda	

[2 marks]

2 1   **En el instituto**

Tu amiga Samanta habla de su instituto.

¿Qué menciona Samanta?

A	Deportes
B	Castigos
C	Transporte público
D	Recreo
E	Profesores
F	Exámenes
G	Comida
H	Reglas

Escribe la letra correcta en cada casilla.

[4 marks]

END OF QUESTIONS

Answers and mark schemes

AQA GCSE Spanish Foundation Practice Papers © Oxford University Press 2020. Photocopying prohibited.

AQA GCSE Spanish (9-1)

PRACTICE PAPER

F

Foundation Tier Paper 2 Speaking

Time allowed: 7–9 minutes
(+12 minutes' supervised preparation time)

Candidate's material – Role-play and Photo card

Instructions

- During the preparation time you must prepare the Role-play card and Photo card given to you.
- You may make notes during the preparation time on the paper provided by your teacher-examiner. Do not write on the stimulus cards.
- Hand your notes and both stimulus cards to the teacher-examiner before the General Conversation.
- You must ask the teacher-examiner at least one question in the General Conversation.

Information

- The test will last a maximum of 9 minutes and will consist of a Role-play (approximately 2 minutes) and a Photo card (approximately 2 minutes), followed by a General Conversation (3–5 minutes) based on your nominated Theme and the remaining Theme which has not been covered in the Photo card.
- You must **not** use a dictionary at any time during the test. This includes the preparation time.

Teacher Part

Please note: The Practice Paper questions and answers have not been written or approved by AQA.

ROLE-PLAY 1

CANDIDATE'S ROLE

Part 1

Instructions to candidates

Your teacher will play the part of a job interviewer in Spain and will speak first.

You should address the interviewer as *usted*.

When you see this – **!** – you will have to respond to something you have not prepared.

When you see this – **?** – you will have to ask a question.

Estás hablando con un entrevistador / una entrevistadora para un puesto de trabajo en España.

- Tu personalidad (**un** detalle)

- **!**

- Trabajo en España – **una** razón

- **?** – Dinero

- Universidad – tu opinión

For each bullet point, all of the language you use is marked, up to the point when the task is accomplished. Anything you say after that point is ignored. If you first say something which is wrong and follow it with a correct response, only 1 mark out of 2 is awarded for communication, as communication has been delayed. The incorrect part of the message is also considered when awarding the knowledge and use of language mark. This means that for each bullet point, what you say first is very important.

ROLE-PLAY 2

CANDIDATE'S ROLE

Part 1

Instructions to candidates

Your teacher will play the part of your Mexican friend and will speak first.

You should address your friend as *tú*.

When you see this – **!** – you will have to respond to something you have not prepared.

When you see this – **?** – you will have to ask a question.

Estás hablando con tu amigo mexicano / tu amiga mexicana sobre las relaciones personales.

- Descripción física de un amigo / una amiga (**dos** detalles)
- **Una** actividad con tu amigo / tu amiga
- **!**
- **?** Novio/novia
- Tu opinión sobre el matrimonio

- At Foundation Tier, you are generally only required to provide one detail for each bullet point, but you may occasionally be required to provide two. Answer each bullet point in full, making sure you have used a verb correctly.
- Carefully read through the role-play scenario and use the preparation time to think about what you might be asked in the surprise (!) question: here it is likely to be something related to your friend or a relationship.

ROLE-PLAY 3

CANDIDATE'S ROLE

Part 1

Instructions to candidates

Your teacher will play the part of an assistant in a Spanish train station and will speak first.

You should address the assistant as *usted*.

When you see this – **!** – you will have to respond to something you have not prepared.

When you see this – **?** – you will have to ask a question.

Estás hablando con el empleado / la empleada de una estación de tren en España.

- Tren – destino

- **!**

- Billete – tipo (**un** detalle)

- **?** Descuento para estudiantes

- Tu viaje – por qué (**una** razón)

- Errors can cost you marks for both Communication and Knowledge and use of language, so keep it simple and don't go beyond the requirements of the task.
- In the Foundation Tier role-plays you are not required to use a past or future tense, but make sure all present-tense verbs you use are correctly formed.

Card A   **Candidate's Photo card**

Part 2

- Look at the photo during the preparation period.

- Make any notes you wish to on an additional piece of paper.

- Your teacher will then ask you questions about the photo and about topics related to **technology in everyday life**.

Your teacher will ask you the following three questions and then **two more questions** which you have not prepared.

- ¿Qué hay en la foto?

- ¿Cuál es tu opinión sobre los móviles? … ¿Por qué?

- ¿Cómo usaste Internet la semana pasada?

- Answering the two unprepared questions can be very daunting. Make sure you know common question words such as *¿cuándo?*, *¿cuántos?*, *¿cuál?*, *¿dónde?*, *¿quién?*, *¿cómo?*, *¿por qué?* and *¿qué?* Keep calm, listen carefully and take your time.
- For a mark in the top band, you will have to answer and develop at least three (i.e. 'most') answers, as well as answer all five questions clearly, and give and explain at least one opinion.

Card B   **Candidate's Photo card**

Part 2

- Look at the photo during the preparation period.

- Make any notes you wish to on an additional piece of paper.

- Your teacher will then ask you questions about the photo and about topics related to **home, town, neighbourhood and region**.

Your teacher will ask you the following three questions and then **two more questions** which you have not prepared.

- ¿Qué hay en la foto?

- ¿Cuáles son tus tiendas favoritas? … ¿Por qué?

- ¿Dónde te gustaría vivir en el futuro?

> - There is a time limit of two minutes in the Photo card section of the Foundation speaking exam. In the 12 minutes' preparation time, you will need to spend more time on the Photo card than the role-play. Try to prepare answers of at least three sentences for each bullet, using a verb in each sentence. In addition, try to anticipate what the surprise questions might be.
> - Don't worry if your answers to the surprise questions are shorter – you haven't had time to prepare these.

Card C　　　**Candidate's Photo card**

Part 2

- Look at the photo during the preparation period.

- Make any notes you wish to on an additional piece of paper.

- Your teacher will then ask you questions about the photo and about topics related to **jobs, career choices and ambitions**.

Your teacher will ask you the following three questions and then **two more questions** which you have not prepared.

- ¿Qué hay en la foto?

- ¿Cuál es tu opinión sobre trabajar en una oficina?

- ¿Te gustaría ir a la universidad? … ¿Por qué (no)?

> Make sure you do lots of Photo card practice. Over time, you will notice that Photo cards on the same topic area often have similar questions and they will all have one question in either a past or future tense. It is much easier to answer questions you have practised before than have to think of something new in the limited preparation time you have before you enter the exam!

GENERAL CONVERSATION

Part 3

The Photo card is followed by a General Conversation. The first part of the conversation will be on a theme nominated by the candidate and the second part on the other theme not covered by the Photo card. The total time for the General Conversation will be between **three and five minutes** and a similar amount of time should be spent on each theme. Here is a reminder of the three themes:

- Identity and culture

- Local, national, international and global areas of interest

- Current and future study and employment

The following pages show two examples of the general conversation with accompanying commentary on how these conversations would be marked, followed by tasks. You can find two further conversations in the model answers document that accompanies this paper.

Conversation 1: Themes 2 and 3

Y ahora la conversación. Empezamos con el tema dos. ¿Dónde vives?
Vivo en un pueblo.

Describe el pueblo.
Es pequeño, es antiguo y me gusta.

Háblame de tu casa.
Vivo en una casa pequeña en el centro del pueblo.

¿Qué hay en cada planta de tu casa?
–

¿Qué habitaciones hay en tu casa?
–

¿Tienes muchos dormitorios?
Mi casa tiene tres dormitorios.

¿Te gusta tu dormitorio?
No, porque es pequeño y antiguo.

¿Qué hay en tu dormitorio?
–

¿Tienes un armario, una cama, una mesa, por ejemplo?
Sí, tengo una cama y una mesa.

¿Dónde te gustaría vivir en el futuro?
Me gustaría vivir en Madrid.

¿Por qué?
Porque es muy grande y divertido.

¿Qué hay en Madrid?
–

¿Hay problemas medioambientales y sociales donde vives?
Sí, hay muchos problemas. Hay contaminación.

Cambiamos de tema y ahora es el tema tres. ¿Qué asignaturas estudias?
–

¿Estudias inglés, matemáticas, historia, por ejemplo?
Sí, estudio inglés, español, música, historia, ciencias, alemán y matemáticas.

¿Cuál es tu asignatura favorita?
Me gusta mucho la música.

¿Por qué te gusta la música?
Porque es muy fácil y divertida. Toco el piano.

¿Hay alguna asignatura que no te gusta?
No me gusta la educación física.

¿Por qué no te gusta?
El profesor es antipático.

En general, ¿cómo son los profesores de tu instituto?
Antipáticos y estrictos.

Describe tu uniforme escolar.
Llevo una chaqueta, unos pantalones negros y una corbata.

¿Crees que el uniforme es una buena idea?
–

¿Cuál es tu opinión sobre tu uniforme?
El uniforme es malo.

¿Qué reglas hay en tu instituto?
–

¿Hay actividades extraescolares en tu instituto?
–

¿Tienes alguna pregunta para mí?
–

Marks and commentary

	Communication	Range and accuracy of language	Pronunciation and intonation	Spontaneity and fluency	Total
Marks	5 (6-1)/10	5/10	2/5	2/5	14/30

This conversation has been given 5 marks for Communication because short responses are consistently given and there are questions that are left unanswered. Opinions are given, but they are not explained. A mark is deducted for not asking a question, even when prompted.

5 marks are gained for Range and accuracy of language. Although the language is accurate, the structures used are simple and repetitive. Information is often given in the form of a list and sometimes the vocabulary provided in the question is simply repeated in the answer.

Pronunciation and intonation have been assumed to be quite inconsistent and anglicised in this instance, and so a mark of 2 is achieved.

For Spontaneity and fluency, it is clear that some limited pre-learned material has been used. Nine questions are left unanswered, so the spontaneity mark is 2.

1. In the conversation, highlight any adjectives that have been repeated by the candidate. What would you replace them with to gain a higher mark for Range and accuracy of language?

2. Complete the conversation by answering the final three questions: firstly, describe the rules in your school; secondly, explain what extracurricular activities there are; and finally, write a question for the teacher-examiner.

Conversation 2: Themes 2 and 3

Y ahora la conversación. Empezamos con el tema dos. ¿Dónde vives?
Vivo en una ciudad en el noroeste de Inglaterra desde hace ocho años.

¿Cómo es tu ciudad?
Es una ciudad típica – grande, ruidosa, pero bastante cultural. Hay monumentos. En el pasado vivía en un pueblo.

¿Cómo era este pueblo?
Era pequeño y bastante tranquilo.

¿Hay problemas sociales o medioambientales donde vives?
Sí, hay violencia y personas sin techo. Además, hay mucho tráfico.

Háblame de tu casa.
Vivo en una casa en el centro de la ciudad. La casa tiene ocho habitaciones. Mi habitación favorita es mi dormitorio.

¿Por qué?
Mi dormitorio es cómodo.

¿Qué hay en tu dormitorio?
Hay una cama blanca a la derecha del armario y una estantería antigua.

¿Dónde te gustaría vivir en el futuro?
Me gustaría vivir en Londres porque es más interesante.

¿Cuáles son las desventajas de vivir en Londres?
–

¿Hay problemas en Londres?
Sí, es una ciudad cara.

Cambiamos de tema y ahora es el tema tres. ¿Qué asignaturas estudias?
En mi instituto estudio ocho asignaturas. Mi asignatura favorita es la química.

¿Por qué es tu asignatura favorita?
Es fácil y muy útil.

¿Qué vas a estudiar el año que viene?
Voy a estudiar química, física y biología.

¿Cómo son los profesores de tu instituto?
Muchos son simpáticos, pero hay dos que son muy estrictos.

¿Qué reglas hay en tu instituto?
Hay muchas reglas. No se debe comer chicle, no se debe correr por los pasillos. Se debe llevar uniforme.

¿Te gusta tu uniforme?
No. Es tonto y feo. ¿Cuál es tu opinión?

A mí me gusta el uniforme. ¿Hiciste alguna actividad extraescolar la semana pasada?
Sí, un club de fotografía.

¿Qué hiciste en el club de fotografía?
–

Marks and commentary

	Communication	Range and accuracy of language	Pronunciation and intonation	Spontaneity and fluency	Total
Marks	8/10	9/10	5/5	5/5	27/30

This conversation has been given 8 marks for Communication because extended responses are occasionally given and a range of opinions is shared. The question asked is suitable, and with a little more detail at times and all questions answered, full marks could be given.

9 marks are awarded for Range and accuracy of language. The range of vocabulary has been improved, with more ambitious topic vocabulary such as *personas sin*

techo ('homeless people') and three tenses are used successfully. A little more detail in some answers would allow further language skills to be showcased for the full 10 marks.

Pronunciation and intonation have been assumed to be generally good and so the 5 marks are given.

For Spontaneity and fluency, 5 marks are also awarded. The conversation flows naturally, with all but two questions answered without hesitation. Any pre-learned material is integrated well into the conversation.

1. In the conversation find two examples of:

    •   verbs in a past tense

    •   verbs in the near future tense.

2. Extend all of the answers that include a past or near future tense. Try to add more verbs in these tenses, along with some ambitious vocabulary.

Model answers and mark schemes

F

Foundation Tier Paper 3 Reading

Time allowed: 45 minutes

Instructions

- Answer **all** questions.
- Answer the questions in the spaces provided.
- In **Section A**, answer the questions in **English**. In **Section B**, answer the questions in **Spanish**. In **Section C**, translate the passage into **English**.
- Cross through any work you do not want to be marked.

Information

- The marks for the questions are shown in brackets.
- The maximum mark for this paper is 60.
- You must **not** use a dictionary.

Please note: The Practice Paper questions and answers have not been written or approved by AQA.

Section A   Questions and answers in **English**

| 0 | 1 |

Local heroes

On a Mexican website you read this news item about local volunteers.

> Los habitantes de La Cascada en México quieren combatir los problemas sociales que hay en su barrio. Estos voluntarios no están jubilados y no pertenecen a ningún grupo religioso. Son jóvenes sensatos y dinámicos que quieren tomar acción directa para mejorar su zona local.

How are the volunteers described?

Write the correct letters in the boxes.

> • Multiple-choice questions are designed to really test your comprehension skills as many or all of the answers can seem possible.
> • Before you sit your exams, make sure you have access to plenty of reading tasks such as these that try to trick you, and perfect your technique of spotting distractors and 'false friends' (i.e. Spanish words that look like English words, but have a different meaning)!

A	sensible
B	old
C	religious
D	sociable
E	retired
F	dynamic
G	sensitive
H	young

[   ] [   ] [   ]

[3 marks]

0 2 Carmina and her teachers

You receive an email from Carmina, a Spanish student you met during an exchange trip to Spain.

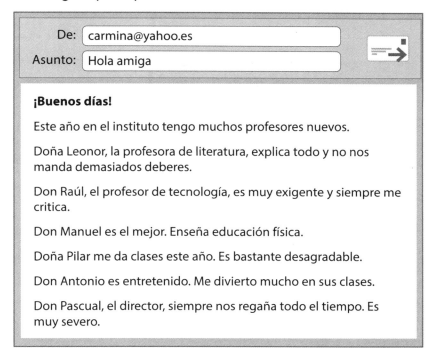

De: carmina@yahoo.es

Asunto: Hola amiga

¡Buenos días!

Este año en el instituto tengo muchos profesores nuevos.

Doña Leonor, la profesora de literatura, explica todo y no nos manda demasiados deberes.

Don Raúl, el profesor de tecnología, es muy exigente y siempre me critica.

Don Manuel es el mejor. Enseña educación física.

Doña Pilar me da clases este año. Es bastante desagradable.

Don Antonio es entretenido. Me divierto mucho en sus clases.

Don Pascual, el director, siempre nos regaña todo el tiempo. Es muy severo.

Who are Carmen's **three** favourite teachers?

Write the correct letters in the boxes.

A	Doña Leonor
B	Don Raúl
C	Don Manuel
D	Doña Pilar
E	Don Antonio
F	Don Pascual

[3 marks]

0 3   *Yerma*, **a play by Federico García Lorca**

Read these stage directions from the play.

Answer the questions that follow.

> Hay una extraña luz de sueño. Un pastor* mira fijamente a Yerma. Lleva de la mano a un niño vestido de blanco. Suena el reloj. Cuando sale el pastor, la luz azul se cambia por una alegre luz de mañana de primavera. Yerma se despierta.

*un pastor – a shepherd

Write the correct letter in each box.

0 3 . 1   The shepherd is…

A	staring at Yerma.
B	feeling tired.
C	acting strangely.

[1 mark]

0 3 . 2   The child is…

A	wearing a dress.
B	holding Yerma's hand.
C	dressed in white.

[1 mark]

0 3 . 3   The scene takes place in…

A	spring.
B	summer.
C	autumn.

[1 mark]

0 3 . 4   Yerma is…

A	getting dressed.
B	falling asleep.
C	waking up.

[1 mark]

0 4   **A football team**

While in a shop in Spain you see an advert for a football team.

¿Tienes menos de dieciocho años?
¿Te apasiona el fútbol? ¡Te necesitamos!

El próximo agosto formaremos el nuevo joven equipo.

Si te interesa:
– Primero, rellena la solicitud en Internet.
– Luego, te haremos una entrevista por teléfono.
– Por último, te invitaremos a una sesión de entrenamiento.

Nuestra ambición es ganar la liga local dentro de tres años.

Answer the questions in **English**.

- Make sure you pay attention to the number of marks available, indicated in brackets. Although many questions are worth one mark, some are worth two or more.
- It pays to remember that the questions follow the order of the text, so the answer to 4.1 is likely to be found in the text at the top of the advert, the answer to 4.2 in the middle, and so on.

0 4 . 1   How old must you be to join the team?

_____

[1 mark]

0 4 . 2   What happens once you have filled in the online application form?

Mention **two** things.

_____

[2 marks]

0 4 . 3   What is the team's ambition?

_____

[1 mark]

| 0 | 5 | **Holidays in Ushuaia**

You are reading this article in an Argentinian newspaper.

El aumento del turismo en Ushuaia

El número de turistas en Ushuaia, una ciudad en el extremo sur de Argentina, ha aumentado más del doble en el último año. Entre los motivos de esta subida se encuentran los bajos precios de los hoteles, la belleza de los parques de la ciudad y, sobre todo, la construcción del nuevo aeropuerto de la ciudad.

Muchos famosos vienen a Ushuaia a esquiar y su influencia en las redes sociales como Instagram y YouTube causará que cada vez más gente joven también venga en el futuro.

Many exam questions require you to identify a specific piece of information hidden among lots of detail, such as the 'main reason', the 'best/worst aspect', etc. This information will often, though not always, come at the end of the paragraph. For example, in 5.1, focus on the information that comes after *sobre todo* ('above all') as you are asked for the main reason for the rise in tourism.

| 0 | 5 |.| 1 | According to the article, what is the **main** reason for the rise in tourism in Ushuaia?

A	cheap hotels
B	beautiful parks
C	the airport

[1 mark]

| 0 | 5 |.| 2 | Who will be **more** likely to visit Ushuaia in the future?

A	celebrities
B	young people
C	YouTubers

[1 mark]

0 6   **A new vocational course**

Your Peruvian friend sends you a link to an advert about a new course in hotel management.

Read the advert.

El Instituto de Estudios Superiores de Lima

Ofrecemos un nuevo curso de hostelería que incluye prácticas en un hotel de lujo.

El hotel tiene piscina interior, servicio de canguro y wifi gratuito.

El curso durará tres meses y medio en total.

Answer the questions in **English**.

Example   What facilities does the hotel offer?

<u>Indoor pool</u>

0 6 . 1   Write **two** more facilities the hotel offers.

_____

[2 marks]

0 6 . 2   How long will the course last in total?

_____

[1 mark]

| 0 | 7 |

Sport

You are reading an interview with Isidora, a Chilean sprinter, in an online newspaper.

- **Isidora, ¿cuál ha sido el momento más memorable de tu carrera?**
- Hasta ahora, está claro que cuando llevé la bandera de Chile en la ceremonia de los Juegos Panamericanos, fue muy emocionante e inolvidable.

- **¿Cuál es tu objetivo este año?**
- Suelo entrenar todos los días para ir a los Juegos Olímpicos el año que viene. Competí muy bien en las pruebas nacionales hace tres meses, pero la competición olímpica será complicada. Las corredoras de Italia y Alemania son las favoritas.

- **¿Participarás en otras competiciones?**
- Quiero dedicarme totalmente en exclusiva a las Olimpiadas, quiero que Chile esté orgulloso de mí.

When does each event take place?

Write   **P** for something that happened in the **past**.

N for something that is happening **now**.

F for something that is going to happen in the **future**.

Write the correct letter in each box.

| 0 | 7 | . | 1 | Carrying the Chilean flag | | **[1 mark]**

| 0 | 7 | . | 2 | Training | | **[1 mark]**

| 0 | 7 | . | 3 | National trials | | **[1 mark]**

| 0 | 7 | . | 4 | Olympic Games | | **[1 mark]**

| 0 8 | **Las Fiestas de la Vendimia, a traditional festival in Valdepeñas, Spain** |

A group of your Spanish friends are going to the festival.

Read their social media posts.

Write the letter of the correct person in each box.

A   Lo mejor de la fiesta es la comida, especialmente la del mercado medieval donde hay carnes y pasteles tradicionales que saben muy rico. **Marisa**

B   Parece que este año el concierto de rock será el evento más concurrido. No quedan entradas. **Carlos**

C   En el mercado medieval no solo hay comida; la ropa y los complementos que venden ahí, siempre llaman mi atención. **Elvira**

D   Voy a ir a la feria equina. Nos encanta ver como se mueven los caballos al ritmo de la música. ¡Es impresionante! **Raúl**

E   Tengo ganas de ayudar a hacer la paella al aire libre en la Plaza Mayor. ¡Me divierto mucho! **Gloria**

- Be aware of key words in the questions such as 'horse' or 'entry' here. Try thinking of words in Spanish that look or sound similar. For example, you might remember *equitación* is 'horse-riding', which is linked to (D) *equina* (meaning 'equine').
- Many words that appear difficult to understand often contain clues within them that can help lead you to the correct answer, for example, (B) *entrada* > *entrar* ('to enter'); (E) *me divierto* > *divertido* ('amusing').

| 0 8 . 1 | Who is looking forward to watching the horse parade? | | **[1 mark]** |

| 0 8 . 2 | Who fears they may not be able to gain entry to part of the festival? | | **[1 mark]** |

| 0 8 . 3 | Who enjoys cooking outside? | | **[1 mark]** |

| 0 8 . 4 | Who is really impressed by the accessories on sale? | | **[1 mark]** |

0	9

A news item about Las Fiestas de la Vendimia in Valdepeñas

You read an article online with more information about this festival.

En esta feria no hay normas estrictas sobre vestuario, pero muchos valdepeñeros llevan ropa tradicional como por ejemplo faldas largas de colores rojos, blancos y amarillos, pantalones negros y decoraciones para el pelo. No está bien visto llevar ropa informal, como pantalones cortos y chanclas.
En la feria sirven comida tradicional como gambas. El queso manchego también es popular. No obstante, su producto estrella es el vino tinto. Si quieres cenar en un restaurante popular, es esencial reservar una mesa con varias semanas de antelación.

Write the correct letter in the boxes.

- Similar to Question 5, this is another extended text with only 2 marks on offer, so you can safely assume there is superfluous information that can be disregarded.
- In the case of 9.1, the information you need regarding what not to wear comes at the end of the first paragraph, after a long list of clothes that locals do wear.
- A good cultural knowledge can be very useful in certain reading tasks, but you should avoid writing an answer based on your own knowledge – always refer closely to the text.

0	9	.	1

What are tourists advised to avoid wearing to the festival?

A	Skirts
B	Trousers
C	Shorts

[1 mark]

0	9	.	2

Which is the most important product of Valdepeñas?

A	Prawns
B	Cheese
C	Wine

[1 mark]

| 1 | 0 | | **Healthy eating** |

Your Spanish friend sends you a message with ingredients for a healthy salad.

> **¡Hola!**
> Estos son los ingredientes que necesitas para hacer mi ensalada súper sana:
>
> Un paquete de tomates pequeños, dos cebollas rojas, cien gramos de judías verdes, una bolsa de patatas nuevas y una lata de aceitunas negras.
> ¡Hasta luego! Paca

Answer the questions in **English**.

What do you need to make the salad?

Example   A packet of…   <u>small tomatoes</u>.

| 1 | 0 | . | 1 | Two… |

_____

[1 mark]

| 1 | 0 | . | 2 | 100g of… |

_____

[1 mark]

| 1 | 0 | . | 3 | A bag of… |

_____

[1 mark]

| 1 | 0 | . | 4 | A tin of… |

_____

[1 mark]

Section B   Questions and answers in **Spanish**

| 1 | 1 | **Información ambiental de Madrid**

Completa el texto usando las palabras de la lista.

Escribe la letra correcta en cada casilla.

> - Gap-fill tasks often require a good knowledge of higher-level vocabulary. The challenge here is to understand the meaning of the sentences so that you can identify the correct infinitive to insert.
> - Aim to work out the meaning gradually from context and by ruling out the more unlikely options. Start by looking carefully at the words on either side of each gap and 'testing out' each verb to see if one sounds sensible.

En la capital de España hay miles de contenedores para [   ] plástico y vidrio.

Este mes los coches no pueden [   ] por las avenidas principales.

El ayuntamiento quiere [   ] la calidad de aire en el centro de la ciudad.

A	circular
B	hacer
C	reciclar
D	contaminar
E	ser
F	mejorar

[   ] [   ] [   ]

[3 marks]

| 1 | 2 | | **Las asignaturas preferidas de los jóvenes** |

Lee lo que dicen.

¿Qué asignatura prefiere cada persona?

A	Educación física
B	Español
C	Geografía
D	Cocina
E	Matemáticas
F	Historia
G	Música
H	Dibujo

Escribe la letra correcta en cada casilla.

| 1 | 2 | . | 1 | | Nuestro planeta me fascina. Me encanta estudiar sus diferentes paisajes y las sociedades que lo habitan. **Gema** |

[1 mark]

| 1 | 2 | . | 2 | | Ahora se me dan bien las operaciones numéricas, las sumas y las restas. También me interesan las figuras geométricas. **Jordi** |

[1 mark]

| 1 | 2 | . | 3 | | Hablo castellano bastante bien. Es un idioma muy útil y me encanta la cultura hispana. **Patricia** |

[1 mark]

| 1 | 2 | . | 4 | | Voy mejor al memorizar fechas y datos importantes. Es importante aprender sobre los eventos importantes del pasado. **Hashim** |

[1 mark]

1 3   *Pepita Jiménez*, **una novela de Juan Valera**

Lee el extracto.

> Don Gumersindo, muy aseado y cuidadoso de su persona, era un viejo que no inspiraba repugnancia.
>
> Las prendas de su sencillo vestuario estaban algo raídas, y de tiempo inmemorial se le conocía la misma capa, el mismo chaquetón y los mismos pantalones y chaleco.
>
> Don Gumersindo tenía excelentes cualidades: era afable, servicial, compasivo, y se desvivía por complacer y ser útil a cualquier persona, aunque le costase trabajo, desvelos y fatiga.
>
> Ya he dicho que era tío de la Pepita. Cuando frisaba en los ochenta años, iba ella a cumplir los dieciséis.

Termina las frases con la palabra correcta.

Escribe la letra correcta en cada casilla.

> - Always be on the lookout for synonyms as they will often lead you to the correct answer, *cuidadoso* > *higiénica*, for example.
> - Avoid distractors – the most obvious option is rarely the right one! In 13.1, you might link *repugnante* to *repugnancia*, but fail to spot the negative *no*.
> - Look for clues, such as repetition of *mismo/misma/mismos* ('same'), followed by words that appear to be clothes (*chaquetón*, *pantalones*). This may help lead you to the correct answer for 13.2 – what did Don Gumersindo never change?

1 3 . **1**   Don Gumersindo era una persona…

A	repugnante.
B	higiénica.
C	desordenada.

[1 mark]

| 1 | 3 |.| 2 | Don Gumersindo nunca cambiaba su…

A	expresión.
B	opinión.
C	ropa.

[1 mark]

| 1 | 3 |.| 3 | Don Gumersindo se comportaba de manera muy atenta con…

A	todo el mundo.
B	la familia real.
C	sus trabajadores.

[1 mark]

| 1 | 3 |.| 4 | Pepita tenía…

A	catorce años.
B	ochenta años.
C	dieciséis anos.

[1 mark]

| 1 | 4 |

El acoso escolar

Mira estos comentarios sobre el acoso escolar de dos estudiantes guatemaltecos.

Omar
No tengo problemas de acoso en mi centro educativo, pero me preocupa que otros estudiantes sufran en silencio, sobre todo los estudiantes más jóvenes. Mi instituto debe crear un grupo de apoyo a las víctimas de acoso.

Marieta
Mi instituto tiene una asociación de estudiantes mayores de dieciséis años que aconseja a los estudiantes sobre los peligros del acoso. Sin embargo, me gustaría que los profesores también intentasen ayudar a la asociación más a menudo.

Contesta a las preguntas en **español**.

| 1 | 4 | . | 1 | ¿De qué se preocupa Omar?

_____

[1 mark]

| 1 | 4 | . | 2 | ¿Qué recomienda Omar?

_____

[1 mark]

| 1 | 4 | . | 3 | Según Marieta, ¿de qué sirve la asociación de estudiantes mayores?

_____

[1 mark]

| 1 | 4 | . | 4 | ¿Qué podrían hacer los profesores en el instituto de Marieta?

_____

[1 mark]

1 5 **Planes familiares**

Lees esta página web sobre planes familiares.

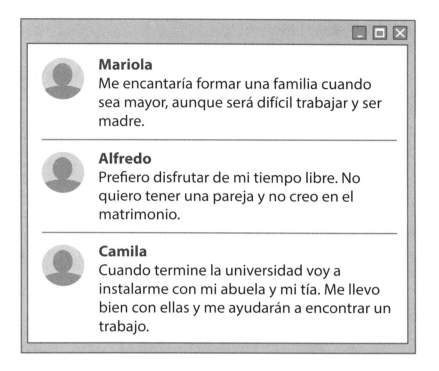

Mariola
Me encantaría formar una familia cuando sea mayor, aunque será difícil trabajar y ser madre.

Alfredo
Prefiero disfrutar de mi tiempo libre. No quiero tener una pareja y no creo en el matrimonio.

Camila
Cuando termine la universidad voy a instalarme con mi abuela y mi tía. Me llevo bien con ellas y me ayudarán a encontrar un trabajo.

¿Qué planes tienen estos jóvenes?

A	Casarse
B	Vivir con su familia extensa
C	Tener hijos
D	Divorciarse
E	Estar soltero

1 5 . 1 Mariola ☐ **[1 mark]**

1 5 . 2 Alfredo ☐ **[1 mark]**

1 5 . 3 Camila ☐ **[1 mark]**

Section C   Translation into **English**

| 1 | 6 | Your Spanish exchange partner sends you this message.

Translate it into **English** for a friend.

> - When revising, as well as learning topic vocabulary, it is also a good idea to include key verbs in a range of tenses (as more than one tense will come up in the translation), common adjectives and verbs of opinion.
> - Always try to leave enough time in your exam to read over your answer carefully at the end and check the quality of English.

> Vivo en un piso pequeño con mis padres y mi hermanastro. Nuestro barrio es bastante bonito y no hay muchos problemas medioambientales. Lo malo es que necesitamos más espacios verdes. El jueves pasado mis amigos jugaron en el parque, pero ¿será eso posible en el futuro?

[9 marks]

_____

_____

_____

_____

_____

_____

_____

_____

END OF QUESTIONS

Answers and mark schemes

PRACTICE PAPER

F

Foundation Tier Paper 4 Writing

Time allowed: 1 hour

Instructions

- You must answer **four** questions.
- You must answer Question 1, Question 2 and Question 3.
- You must answer **either** Question 4.1 **or** Question 4.2. Do not answer **both** of these questions.
- Answer all questions in **Spanish**.
- Answer the questions in the spaces provided.
- Cross through any work you do not want to be marked.

Information

- The marks for the questions are shown in brackets.
- The maximum mark for this paper is 50.
- You must **not** use a dictionary during this test.
- In order to score the highest marks for Question 4.1/Question 4.2, you must write something about each bullet point. You must use a variety of vocabulary and structures and include your opinions.

Please note: The Practice Paper questions and answers have not been written or approved by AQA.

Answer the questions in the spaces provided.

0 1 Decides enviar esta foto por WhatsApp a un amigo colombiano.

¿Qué hay en la foto? Escribe cuatro frases en **español**.

> • Marks in this question are for communication only: clarity of the message is the key element, so you will be most successful if you use simple, clear language.
> • It is a good idea to learn a small list of expressions and key verbs that can be applied to almost any photo. These could include: *veo* ('I see'), *hay* ('there is/are'), *es* ('he/she/it is'), *tiene* ('he/she/it has') and *parece* ('he/she/it seems').
> • Don't talk about what's not in the photo as this will score zero marks. Sentences have to relate to something that is in the photo, so giving a general opinion such as *me gusta la foto* will not be given credit either.

0 1 . 1

_____

[2 marks]

0 1 . 2

_____

[2 marks]

| 0 | 1 |.| 3 |

_____

[2 marks]

| 0 | 1 |.| 4 |

_____

[2 marks]

0 2   Tu amigo español, Jaime, te ha preguntado sobre tu pueblo.

Escríbele un email.

Menciona:

- tus sitios favoritos

- lo malo de tu pueblo

- tu casa

- tu dormitorio.

Escribe aproximadamente **40** palabras en **español**.

[16 marks]

> - You can stick to the present tense when covering the four bullet points in question 2, as knowledge of past or future tenses is not being tested.
> - The first and second bullets require an opinion, so try to use a range of verb structures and vocabulary in your answer to gain higher marks.
> - Stick to what you know and try to avoid being overambitious with your sentences. This question is testing variety and control of language rather than complexity.
> - If you have time at the end of the exam, check the verbs and spellings in your answer as carefully as possible.

0 3   Translate the following sentences into **Spanish**.

> - If you are finding some of the sentences in question 3 difficult, don't give up! Each sentence is broken down into two or three parts, so you can still gain marks for conveying key messages by giving partial answers.
> - Your mark for application of grammatical knowledge of language and structures can be improved by showing a willingness to guess, as more credit is given to candidates who make an attempt over those who leave gaps.
> - If you do not know a word or phrase, try to think of an alternative that might work in its place. You may not know 'party' (*fiesta*), for instance, but remember the word 'celebration' (*celebración*), which would be credited, whereas leaving it blank will not.

I don't like sports.

_____

_____

It is very important to recycle paper.

_____

_____

I don't get on well with my sister.

_____

_____

I went to a party last week.

_____

_____

In August, we are going to visit Germany.

_____

_____

[10 marks]

Answer **either** Question 4.1 **or** Question 4.2.
You must **not** answer **both** of these questions.

EITHER Question 4.1

0 4 . 1   Tu amiga colombiana te manda un email sobre su familia.

Respóndele y menciona:

- qué cosas hiciste con tu familia la semana pasada

- con quién te llevas mejor en casa

- si prefieres pasar el fin de semana con tus padres o amigos

- cómo vas a celebrar el cumpleaños de un miembro de tu familia.

Escribe aproximadamente **90** palabras en **español**.
Responde a todos los aspectos de la pregunta.

- You will need to refer to all three time frames in your answer (past, present and future), so check that your verb tenses are accurate.
- You can repeat the language in the bullet to start your sentence (*La semana pasada…*).
- You need to write about more than one activity (*cosas*) that you did; it will not be enough to focus on just one as you won't gain as many marks.

[16 marks]

OR Question 4.2

0 4 . 2   Tu amigo cubano quiere saber qué deportes y actividades haces en tu tiempo libre.

Escríbele un email.

Menciona:

- qué deportes y actividades hiciste el verano pasado

- tu opinión sobre los deportes acuáticos

- qué haces en educación física en el instituto

- qué otras actividades te gustaría hacer en el futuro.

Escribe aproximadamente **90** palabras en **español**.
Responde a todos los aspectos de la pregunta.

- You need to express at least two opinions, avoiding obvious repetition, in order to gain the highest marks. Remember to justify your opinions with reasons as much as possible and try to include conjunctions such as *además*, *porque*, *pero* or *aunque*, to create longer sentences.
- Check which tense you need to be writing in, and remember you can use the language of the bullet points to help structure your response, particularly when you are unsure.

[16 marks]

_____

_____

_____

_____

_____

_____

_____

_____

_____

_____

_____

_____

_____

_____

_____

_____

END OF QUESTIONS

Model answers and mark schemes

AQA GCSE Spanish (9-1)

F

Foundation Tier Paper 1 Listening

Time allowed: 35 minutes
(including 5 minutes' reading time before the test)

You will need no other materials.
The pauses are pre-recorded for this test.

Information
- The marks for the questions are shown in brackets. The maximum mark for this paper is 40.
- You must **not** use a dictionary.

Advice
This is what you should do for each item.
- After the question number is announced, there will be a pause to allow you to read the instructions and questions.
- Listen carefully to the recording and read the questions again.
- Listen to the recording again, and then answer the questions.
- When the next question is about to start you will hear a bleep.
- You may write at any time during the test.
- In **Section A**, answer the questions in **English**. In **Section B**, answer the questions in **Spanish**.
- You must answer all the questions in the spaces provided. Do not write on blank pages.
- Write neatly and put down all the information you are asked to give.
- **You must not ask questions or interrupt during the test.**
- You have five minutes to read through the question paper. You may make notes during this time. You may turn to the questions now.
- **The test starts now.**

Listen to the audio

Please note: The Practice Paper questions and answers have not been written or approved by AQA.

Section A   Questions and answers in **English**

Free time

Two Mexican students are talking to you about what they do at the weekend.

What **two** activities does each person do?

Write the correct letters in the boxes.

A	Cooking
B	Listening to music
C	Playing videogames
D	Clothes shopping
E	Reading
F	Doing homework
G	Downloading music
H	Going to the cinema

0 1   ☐   ☐   **[2 marks]**

0 2   ☐   ☐   **[2 marks]**

Extra-curricular activities in Madrid

While you are visiting a school in Madrid, you listen to the headteacher telling students what extra-curricular activities will be available next week.

Which **two** activities does he mention?

Write the correct letters in the boxes.

A	Art workshop
B	Learning a foreign language
C	Creative writing
D	Trip to an art gallery

0 3   ☐   ☐   **[2 marks]**

Extra-curricular activities in Madrid (continued)

Lunchtime options

The headteacher also describes lunch arrangements for the week ahead.

What type of food will be served and in what coloured area of the canteen?

Example   _Vegetarian dishes in the blue area._

0	4

_____

[1 mark]

0	5

_____

[1 mark]

0	6

_____

[1 mark]

| 0 | 7 |

Social issues

You are listening to a podcast where people are discussing social issues that concern them in Spanish cities.

For each speaker, choose their area of concern.

Write the correct letter in each box.

A	Poverty
B	Unemployment
C	Obesity
D	Drug addiction
E	Crime

Answer all parts of the question.

| 0 | 7 | . | 1 | Beatriz   ☐   **[1 mark]**

| 0 | 7 | . | 2 | Nia   ☐   **[1 mark]**

| 0 | 7 | . | 3 | Alberto   ☐   **[1 mark]**

Volunteering in Spain

You hear your Spanish friend, Isabel, talking to her friends about volunteering in the local community.

Complete the sentences in **English**.

| 0 | 8 | This weekend, Isabel needs volunteers to…

_____

[1 mark]

| 0 | 9 | At the end of the day, Isabel would like the volunteers to…

_____

[1 mark]

| 1 | 0 | In return for their help, each volunteer will receive…

_____

[1 mark]

1 **1**   **A year abroad**

Your friend from Santiago de Chile is talking to you about the benefits of a gap year in Japan.

What **three** advantages does he mention?

Answer in **English**.

1 **1** . **1**

_____

[1 mark]

1 **1** . **2**

_____

[1 mark]

1 **1** . **3**

_____

[1 mark]

1 **2**   What **two** pieces of advice does your friend give you?

A	Travel alone
B	Do voluntary work
C	Save up before going
D	Visit only one country

Write the correct letters in the boxes.

☐ ☐

[2 marks]

| 1 | 3 | **Family matters**

You are listening to a Spanish radio programme about modern family life.

For each speaker, choose the issue they are discussing.

Write the correct letter in each box.

A	Loneliness in old age
B	Disobedient children
C	Illness and disability
D	Single-parent families
E	Financial difficulties

Answer all parts of the question.

| 1 | 3 | . | 1 | [1 mark]

| 1 | 3 | . | 2 | [1 mark]

| 1 | 3 | . | 3 | [1 mark]

| 1 | 4 | **A debate about bullfighting**

You are listening to a podcast on Spanish radio about bullfighting.

What is each person's opinion?

Write   **P** for a **positive** opinion.

        N for a **negative** opinion.

        P+N for a **positive** and **negative** opinion.

Write the correct letter(s) in each box.

| 1 | 4 | . | 1 | Adela   [1 mark]

| 1 | 4 | . | 2 | Iker   [1 mark]

| 1 | 4 | . | 3 | Lola   [1 mark]

| 1 | 4 | . | 4 | Hasan   [1 mark]

 AQA GCSE Spanish Foundation Practice Papers © Oxford University Press 2020. Photocopying prohibited.

Environmental issues

While on holiday in La Palma you hear these opinions online about environmental issues.

What does each person say?

Write the correct letter in each box.

1 5

A	Global warming is a serious problem.
B	I'm not worried about global warming.
C	My opinion about global warming has changed.

[1 mark]

1 6

A	There is a lack of recycling containers in Alicante.
B	Alicante recycles more than any other Spanish city.
C	Recycling in Alicante is easy.

[1 mark]

1 7

A	Forest fires are on the increase in Spain.
B	There were fewer forest fires in Spain this year.
C	There is no evidence of forest fires in Spain.

[1 mark]

1 8

A	There is more and more deforestation in Chile.
B	Unfortunately, air quality in Chile is poor.
C	Droughts in Chile are increasingly common.

[1 mark]

1 9

A	What can we do to save species threatened with extinction in Mexico?
B	How many species are currently threatened with extinction in Mexico?
C	Why does no one care that so many species are threatened with extinction in Mexico?

[1 mark]

Section B   Questions and answers in **Spanish**

Los pasatiempos

Escuchas unas entrevistas en la radio española.

¿De qué pasatiempos hablan las personas y cuándo?

Completa la tabla en **español**.

Ejemplo   Nina

Pasatiempo en el pasado	Pasatiempo ahora	Ambición para el futuro
(el) atletismo	baile	ser bailarina profesional

2	0

Fausto

Pasatiempo en el pasado	Pasatiempo ahora	Ambición para el futuro
		escalar las montañas

[2 marks]

2	1

Marta

Pasatiempo en el pasado	Pasatiempo ahora	Ambición para el futuro
	el judo	

[2 marks]

2	2

Las relaciones personales en la familia

Los padres de tu amiga ecuatoriana están hablando sobre las relaciones personales en la familia.

¿Qué van a hacer para llevarse mejor?

A	Acostarse temprano
B	Apagar el móvil
C	Cenar juntos
D	Dar un paseo
E	Dejar de gritar
F	Escuchar a los hijos
G	Ir al cine
H	Ver la tele

Responde a las dos partes de la pregunta.

Escribe la letra correcta en cada casilla.

| 2 | 2 | . | 1 | Según el padre, ¿cómo van a llevarse mejor? | | | **[2 marks]** |

| 2 | 2 | . | 2 | Según la madre, ¿cómo van a llevarse mejor? | | | **[2 marks]** |

END OF QUESTIONS

Answers and mark schemes

PRACTICE PAPER

F

Foundation Tier Paper 2 Speaking

Time allowed: 7–9 minutes
(+12 minutes' supervised preparation time)

Candidate's material – Role-play and Photo card

Instructions

- During the preparation time you must prepare the Role-play card and Photo card given to you.
- You may make notes during the preparation time on the paper provided by your teacher-examiner. Do not write on the stimulus cards.
- Hand your notes and both stimulus cards to the teacher-examiner before the General Conversation.
- You must ask the teacher-examiner at least one question in the General Conversation.

Information

- The test will last a maximum of 9 minutes and will consist of a Role-play (approximately 2 minutes) and a Photo card (approximately 2 minutes), followed by a General Conversation (3–5 minutes) based on your nominated Theme and the remaining Theme which has not been covered in the Photo card.
- You must **not** use a dictionary at any time during the test. This includes the preparation time.

Teacher Part

Please note: The Practice Paper questions and answers have not been written or approved by AQA.

ROLE-PLAY 1

CANDIDATE'S ROLE

Part 1

Instructions to candidates

Your teacher will play the part of your Honduran friend and will speak first.

You should address your friend as *tú*.

When you see this – **!** – you will have to respond to something you have not prepared.

When you see this – **?** – you will have to ask a question.

> Estás hablando con tu amigo hondureño / tu amiga hondureña sobre la tecnología.
>
> - Uso de tu móvil (**una** actividad)
>
> - **!**
>
> - Tu aplicación favorita y **una** razón
>
> - Una desventaja de las redes sociales (**un** detalle)
>
> - **?** Las tabletas

ROLE-PLAY 2

CANDIDATE'S ROLE

Part 1

Instructions to candidates

Your teacher will play the part of the assistant in a tourist office in Barcelona and will speak first.

You should address the assistant as *usted*.

When you see this – **!** – you will have to respond to something you have not prepared.

When you see this – **?** – you will have to ask a question.

Estás hablando con el empleado / la empleada de una oficina de turismo de Barcelona.

- Una excursión – dónde

- **!**

- Viaje – tren o autocar y **una** razón

- **?** Precio

- Tu opinión sobre Barcelona (**un** detalle)

ROLE-PLAY 3

CANDIDATE'S ROLE

Part 1

Instructions to candidates

Your teacher will play the part of a Spanish teacher you have just met while on a Spanish exchange trip.

You should address the teacher as *usted*.

When you see this – **!** – you will have to respond to something you have not prepared.

When you see this – **?** – you will have to ask a question.

Estás hablando con un profesor / una profesora en un instituto español.

- Tu instituto – dónde
- **!**
- Tu asignatura favorita y **una** razón
- Una desventaja del uniforme
- **?** Actividades extraescolares

Card A   **Candidate's Photo card**

Part 2

- Look at the photo during the preparation period.

- Make any notes you wish to on an additional piece of paper.

- Your teacher will then ask you questions about the photo and about topics related to **global issues**.

Your teacher will ask you the following three questions and then **two more questions** which you have not prepared.

- ¿Qué hay en la foto?

- ¿Qué problemas sociales o medioambientales te preocupan?

- ¿Qué vas a hacer para proteger el medio ambiente?

Card B　　**Candidate's Photo card**

Part 2

- Look at the photo during the preparation period.

- Make any notes you wish to on an additional piece of paper.

- Your teacher will then ask you questions about the photo and about topics related to **life at school/college**.

Your teacher will ask you the following three questions and then **two more questions** which you have not prepared.

- ¿Qué hay en la foto?

- ¿Qué opinas de las instalaciones de tu instituto?

- ¿Qué comiste en tu instituto la semana pasada?

Card C   **Candidate's Photo card**

Part 2

- Look at the photo during the preparation period.

- Make any notes you wish to on an additional piece of paper.

- Your teacher will then ask you questions about the photo and about topics related to **customs and festivals in Spanish-speaking countries**.

Your teacher will ask you the following three questions and then **two more questions** which you have not prepared.

- ¿Qué hay en la foto?

- ¿Qué opinas de esta tradición?

- ¿A qué otros festivales hispanos te gustaría ir?

GENERAL CONVERSATION

Part 3

The Photo card is followed by a General Conversation. The first part of the conversation will be on a theme nominated by the candidate and the second part on the other theme not covered by the Photo card. The total time for the General Conversation will be between **three and five minutes** and a similar amount of time should be spent on each theme. Here is a reminder of the three themes:

- Identity and culture

- Local, national, international and global areas of interest

- Current and future study and employment

The following pages show two examples of the general conversation with accompanying commentary on how these conversations would be marked, followed by tasks. You can find two further conversations in the model answers document that accompanies this paper.

Conversation 1: Themes 1 and 3

Y ahora la conversación. Empezamos con el tema uno. ¿Cuál es tu deporte favorito?
Mi deporte favorito es la natación.

¿Cuándo la practicas?
—

¿Practicas la natación todos los días?
Sí, todos los días.

¿Por qué te gusta la natación?
Es fácil.

¿Hay deportes que no te gustan?
Sí, el golf.

¿Por qué?
Porque es aburrido.

¿Qué actividades hiciste el fin de semana pasado?
El cine.

Describe tu visita al cine.
—

¿Con quién fuiste?
Con mi hermano y mis amigos.

¿Por qué te gusta el cine?
El cine es divertido.

¿Cuál es tu película favorita?
Me gustan las películas de ciencia ficción.

¿Qué otros pasatiempos tienes?
–

¿Te gusta leer?
No.

¿Por qué?
Es aburrido.

¿Qué aplicaciones usas?
Uso Instagram y es divertido. Y tú, ¿qué usas?

Uso Twitter a veces. ¿Qué es lo bueno y lo malo de las redes sociales?
Son divertidas.

¿Y lo malo?
–

¿Usas otras aplicaciones?
Sí, uso TikTok.

¿Qué es exactamente?
–

¿Es una red social?
Sí.

Cambiamos de tema y ahora es el tema tres. ¿Tienes un trabajo a tiempo parcial?
No.

¿Ayudas en casa?
–

¿En casa haces tu cama, lavas los platos o pones la mesa?
Sí, lavo los platos.

¿Qué trabajo te gustaría hacer en el futuro?
Me gustaría ser policía.

¿Por qué te gustaría ser policía?
Es muy interesante.

¿Hay desventajas?
–

¿Qué es lo malo de este trabajo?
Es peligroso.

Describe tus prácticas laborales del año pasado.
–

¿Qué hiciste?

–

¿Qué vas a hacer después de los exámenes?

Vacaciones.

¿Cuál es tu asignatura favorita?

Mi asignatura favorita es la geografía, pero no me gusta el inglés.

Describe tu instituto.

Es grande y moderno. Es agradable.

¿Cómo son los profesores?

Simpáticos, inteligentes.

Describe tu uniforme.

Es gris, negro y verde. Es útil.

Marks and commentary

	Communication	Range and accuracy of language	Pronunciation and intonation	Spontaneity and fluency	Total
Marks	4/10	4/10	3/5	2/5	13/30

This conversation has been given 4 marks for Communication because apart from the simpler questions on school life, short responses are given and the examiner is forced to rephrase to such an extent that they give most of the vocabulary required to answer the question. Lots of basic opinions are used, but there are frequent misunderstandings and no attempt at narration.

4 marks are awarded for Range and accuracy of language. Vocabulary is repetitive and there is a severe lack of complex structures. On numerous occasions, the vocabulary of the question is repeated but frequently without a verb.

Pronunciation and intonation have been assumed to be generally understandable and gain 3 marks. For Spontaneity and fluency, it is clear that there is a limited exchange with lots of hesitation and so 2 marks are gained.

1. Re-read the conversation and find any answers that do not contain a verb. Try to insert a suitable verb for each of the answers.

2. Answer the first six questions of this conversation, from *¿Cuál es tu deporte favorito?* ('What is your favourite sport?') to *¿Por qué?* ('Why?'), but merge your answers into one paragraph, using complex structures and vocabulary.

Conversation 2: Themes 1 and 3

Y ahora la conversación. Empezamos con el tema uno. ¿Cuál es tu deporte favorito?
Mi deporte favorito es la natación. La practico todos los días. Me gusta mucho.

¿Por qué te gusta mucho la natación?
Es fácil y muy útil para mantenerme en forma.

¿Hay deportes que no te gustan?
No me interesa el golf porque es demasiado lento.

¿Qué actividades hiciste el fin de semana pasado?
El sábado pasado fui al cine. Vi una película de terror. ¡Fue escalofriante!

¿Prefieres ver las películas en el cine o en casa?
El cine es mucho mejor porque la pantalla es más grande.

¿Qué otros pasatiempos tienes?
Me gusta mucho leer novelas y de vez en cuando veo series de Netflix en mi tableta.

¿Qué aplicaciones usas?
Ahora uso Instagram. Es bastante divertido. Subo fotos una vez al día. Y tú, ¿qué aplicaciones usas?

Uso Twitter a veces. ¿Qué es lo bueno y lo malo de las redes sociales?
Las redes sociales son bastante interesantes porque se puede leer noticias, hablar con amigos y mucho más. Lo malo es que son adictivas y una pérdida de tiempo.

Cambiamos de tema y ahora es el tema tres. ¿Tienes un trabajo a tiempo parcial?
No tengo un trabajo a tiempo parcial, pero ayudo mucho en casa.

¿Qué haces?
Limpio mi habitación, paso la aspiradora y de vez en cuando lavo el coche de mi padre. Me da veinte euros.

¿En qué gastas el dinero?
Siempre ahorro el dinero.

¿Qué trabajo te gustaría hacer en el futuro?
No quiero ir a la universidad. Me gustaría ser policía.

¿Por qué te gustaría ser policía?
Es muy interesante y quiero ayudar a las personas.

¿Hay desventajas?
Pienso que es un poco peligroso en las grandes ciudades.

Describe tus prácticas laborales del año pasado.
Trabajé en una tienda de ropa de cerca de mi casa. Fue un poco aburrido, pero fue una experiencia útil porque ahora soy más extrovertido.

¿Qué vas a hacer después de los exámenes?
Voy a ir de vacaciones luego voy a buscar un trabajo a tiempo parcial, por ejemplo, en un restaurante.

Marks and commentary

	Communication	Range and accuracy of language	Pronunciation and intonation	Spontaneity and fluency	Total
Marks	10/10	10/10	5/5	5/5	30/30

This conversation has been given 10 marks for Communication. Responses are now generally much more detailed. The teacher-examiner is not required to ask many questions to prompt responses. Opinions are much more ambitious, for example *Es muy interesante y quiero ayudar a las personas* ('It is very interesting and I want to help people').

10 marks are awarded for Range and accuracy of language. Although many of the opinion structures are relatively simple, there are numerous attempts at more ambitious structures and vocabulary, such as *escalofriante* ('terrifying') and *pienso que* ('I think that'). Whereas in the first response verbs were often missed out, here three tenses are used confidently and accurately.

Pronunciation and intonation have been assumed to be good, reflecting the level of language used, gaining 5 marks. For Spontaneity and fluency, it is clear that there is good engagement in a very impressive exchange and so the full 5 marks are achieved.

1. Find the following expressions in the conversation:
   - I practise it
   - to keep fit
   - much better
   - a waste of time
   - he gives me
   - I am going to look for

2. Write sentences about either your free-time activities or future plans using at least three of the expressions above.

Model answers and mark schemes

AQA GCSE Spanish (9-1)

F

Foundation Tier Paper 3 Reading

Time allowed: 45 minutes

Instructions

- Answer **all** questions.
- Answer the questions in the spaces provided.
- In **Section A**, answer the questions in **English**. In **Section B**, answer the questions in **Spanish**. In **Section C**, translate the passage into **English**.
- Cross through any work you do not want to be marked.

Information

- The marks for the questions are shown in brackets.
- The maximum mark for this paper is 60.
- You must **not** use a dictionary.

Please note: The Practice Paper questions and answers have not been written or approved by AQA.

Section A   Questions and answers in **English**

| 0 | 1 |

An online profile

You are creating a profile on a Spanish social media app.

A	Nombre
B	Apodo
C	Fecha de nacimiento
D	Lugar de nacimiento
E	Domicilio
F	Correo
G	Contraseña
H	Cualidades
I	Pasatiempos

Write the correct letter in each box.

On which line should you enter:

Example   …your name? | A |

| 0 | 1 |.| 1 | …your place of birth?   [ ]   **[1 mark]**

| 0 | 1 |.| 2 | …your hobbies?   [ ]   **[1 mark]**

| 0 | 1 |.| 3 | …your nickname?   [ ]   **[1 mark]**

| 0 | 1 |.| 4 | …your password?   [ ]   **[1 mark]**

0 2   **Work experience**

Your Spanish friend Iago sends you an email about his recent work experience.

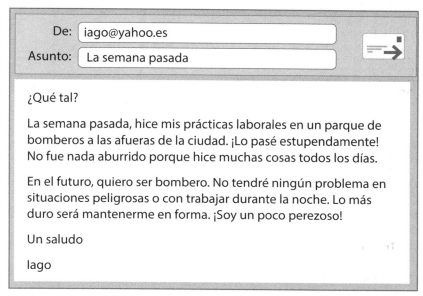

De: iago@yahoo.es

Asunto: La semana pasada

¿Qué tal?

La semana pasada, hice mis prácticas laborales en un parque de bomberos a las afueras de la ciudad. ¡Lo pasé estupendamente! No fue nada aburrido porque hice muchas cosas todos los días.

En el futuro, quiero ser bombero. No tendré ningún problema en situaciones peligrosas o con trabajar durante la noche. Lo más duro será mantenerme en forma. ¡Soy un poco perezoso!

Un saludo

Iago

Write the correct letter in each box.

0 2 . 1   What adjective best describes Iago's work experience?

A	Stupid
B	Great
C	Boring

[1 mark]

0 2 . 2   What will be the hardest thing for Iago?

A	Dangerous situations
B	Working at night
C	Keeping fit

[1 mark]

0 3 **A birthday to remember**

You read this email from your Mexican friend, Fabio, telling you about a family event.

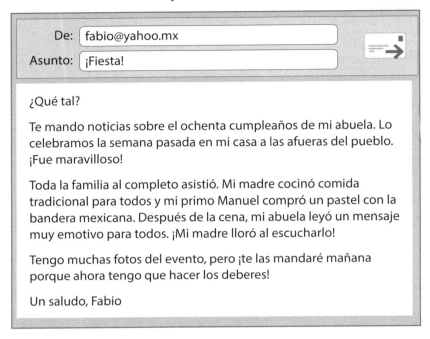

De: fabio@yahoo.mx

Asunto: ¡Fiesta!

¿Qué tal?

Te mando noticias sobre el ochenta cumpleaños de mi abuela. Lo celebramos la semana pasada en mi casa a las afueras del pueblo. ¡Fue maravilloso!

Toda la familia al completo asistió. Mi madre cocinó comida tradicional para todos y mi primo Manuel compró un pastel con la bandera mexicana. Después de la cena, mi abuela leyó un mensaje muy emotivo para todos. ¡Mi madre lloró al escucharlo!

Tengo muchas fotos del evento, pero ¡te las mandaré mañana porque ahora tengo que hacer los deberes!

Un saludo, Fabio

Answer the questions in **English**.

0 3 . 1 Where **exactly** is Fabio's house located?

_____

_____

[1 mark]

0 3 . 2 What was special about the birthday cake Manuel bought?

_____

_____

[1 mark]

0 3 . 3 What did Fabio's grandmother do after dinner?

_____

_____

[1 mark]

0 3 . 4 How did Fabio's mother react?

_____

_____

[1 mark]

0 3 . 5 Why can't Fabio send pictures of the event until tomorrow?

_____

_____

[1 mark]

0 4   **Hobbies**

During a holiday in Valencia you look at this list of activities advertised in your hotel.

Actividades	Información
Compras en el centro	Minibús gratis cada hora
Concierto de rock	¡Solo nos quedan doce entradas!
Natación	Exclusivo para menores de 16 años
Bailes Latinos	A las diez de la noche, los días laborales
Ajedrez	Exclusivo para participantes sin experiencia
Fotografía	Al aire libre. ¡Lleva zapatos cómodos!
Ciclismo	Cada jueves con bicicletas de montaña

Answer the questions in **English**.

According to the list, which activity…

0 4 . 1   … involves a lot of walking?

_____

[1 mark]

0 4 . 2   … is in high demand?

_____

[1 mark]

0 4 . 3   … is only for beginners?

_____

[1 mark]

0 4 . 4   … does not take place at the weekend?

_____

[1 mark]

0 5 **A famous Spanish actress**

You read this article about Spanish actress, Belén in a Spanish magazine.

> **Belén rodará varias películas el año que viene**
>
> La famosa actriz española Belén declaró ayer en una entrevista que el año que viene va a estar muy ocupada con cuatro proyectos: tres nuevas películas y una serie de televisión.
> Belén comentó: "Estoy muy nerviosa, pero tengo muchas ganas de empezar, especialmente la serie, porque el director es un buen amigo mío. Me dijo que tratará sobre el paro en España."

Write the correct letter in each box.

0 5 . 1 How many films is Belén appearing in next year?

A	4
B	3
C	9

[1 mark]

0 5 . 2 Why is she so keen to start filming her new series?

A	She is good friends with the director.
B	The director's company is paying her a lot of money.
C	The director is very highly rated.

[1 mark]

0 5 . 3 What is the series about?

A	Poverty
B	Homelessness
C	Unemployment

[1 mark]

| 0 | 6 | **Using the local library**

You read this blog post online about the importance of local libraries.

Me encanta la biblioteca de mi barrio; es un edificio muy bonito y juega un papel muy importante en nuestra comunidad.

Hace dos días hice los deberes allí en un ambiente silencioso y agradable. ¡Fue ideal!

Pronto mi mejor amigo, Julián, irá a la biblioteca para mandar unos correos electrónicos urgentes.

No tendrá que pagar porque la conexión de wifi es gratis. Mi hermana Marga casi nunca va a la biblioteca, pero ahora está allí consultando una enciclopedia.

Además, el próximo mes de noviembre habrá una charla sobre el manga y me gustaría ir con Julián, porque nos encanta.

When does each event take place?

Write   **P** for something that happened in the **past**.

       N for something that is happening **now**.

       F for something that is going to happen in the **future**.

Write the correct letter in each box.

| 0 | 6 | . | 1 | Doing homework   ☐   **[1 mark]**

| 0 | 6 | . | 2 | Sending emails   ☐   **[1 mark]**

| 0 | 6 | . | 3 | Consulting an encyclopaedia   ☐   **[1 mark]**

| 0 | 6 | . | 4 | Attending a manga discussion group   ☐   **[1 mark]**

0	7

A new school initiative

On a visit to your Spanish exchange partner's school, you see this poster.

> **¡HABLA CON NOSOTROS!**
>
> ¿Te sientes solo a veces?
>
> ¿Sufres acoso escolar?
>
> ¿Quieres relajarte en un ambiente amistoso y sin ruidos?
>
> Puedes venir al aula número 238 y pasar el recreo con nuestro equipo de apoyo al estudiante.

Give three reasons why someone might want to go to classroom 238 at break time.

Answer in **English**.

0	7	.	1

_____

[1 mark]

0	7	.	2

_____

[1 mark]

0	7	.	3

_____

[1 mark]

0	8

***Canto a Andalucía*, a poem by Manuel Machado**

Cádiz, salada claridad. Granada,
agua oculta que llora.
Romana y mora, Córdoba callada.
Málaga cantaora.
Almería, dorada.
Plateado, Jaén. Huelva, la orilla
de las tres carabelas.

Y Sevilla.

A	Golden
B	Pretty
C	Modern
D	Silver-plated
E	Clean
F	Quiet
G	Small

How does the poet describe the following Spanish cities?

Write the correct letter in each box.

| 0 | 8 | . | 1 | Córdoba | [blank box] | **[1 mark]** |

| 0 | 8 | . | 2 | Almería | [blank box] | **[1 mark]** |

| 0 | 8 | . | 3 | Jaén | [blank box] | **[1 mark]** |

0	9

Environment

You are in an Argentinian school with your friend and you see this sign.

> **USA SOLO LA ENERGÍA QUE NECESITES.**
>
> **POR FAVOR, APAGA LAS LUCES.**

Answer the question in **English**.

Example   What is the poster about?   <u>Saving energy</u>.

What does the poster ask you to do?

_____

[1 mark]

1 0   *Luces de Bohemia*, **a play by Ramón del Valle-Inclán**

Read this extract and answer the questions that follow.

MAX:	¿Eres joven? No puedo verte.
EL PRESO:	Soy joven. Treinta años.
MAX:	¿De qué te acusan?
EL PRESO:	Es cuento largo. Soy tachado de rebelde . . . No quise ir a la guerra y levanté una rebelión en la fábrica. Me denunció el patrón, cumplí condena, recorrí el mundo buscando trabajo, y ahora voy por tránsitos, reclamado de no sé qué jueces. Conozco la suerte que me espera: cuatro tiros por intento de fuga.

Write the correct letter in each box.

1 0 . 1   Which statement best describes the prisoner?

A	He is dirty.
B	He is thirty years old.
C	He is blind.

[1 mark]

1 0 . 2   Which adjectives best describe the prisoner?

A	Young and rebellious.
B	Tall and aggressive.
C	Hard-working and lucky.

[1 mark]

1 0 . 3   What is the prisoner accused of?

A	Starting a riot in a factory.
B	Committing war crimes.
C	Attacking the boss.

[1 mark]

1 0 . 4   What is likely to happen to the prisoner?

A	He will be released.
B	He will receive a long prison sentence.
C	He will be executed.

[1 mark]

Section B Questions and answers in **Spanish**

1 1   **El cambio climático y los países latinoamericanos**

Te interesa el cambio climático y lees estos titulares en una página web.

	Impacto del cambio climático en América Latina
A	En Chile, el aumento del nivel de agua en la costa amenaza a la población, sobre todo en Santiago, la capital.
B	En Argentina, los glaciares del sur desaparecen y los pingüinos no tienen un hábitat seguro para reproducirse.
C	En Perú, la sequía en la ciudad de Lima causa deficiencias en el servicio de agua potable en siete barrios de la capital.
D	En Bogotá, la capital de Colombia, la subida de la temperatura media provoca que los pájaros mueran o emigren a otros climas más frescos.
E	En Panamá, la contaminación del aire en la capital produce alergias y problemas respiratorios en los habitantes.
F	Bolivia sufre incendios devastadores en el Amazonas que acaban con cultivos de frutas y verduras.

Tus amigos están interesados en ayudar a las víctimas del cambio climático.

¿Dónde deben ir?

Escribe la letra correcta en cada casilla.

1 1 . 1   Me interesa visitar los lugares más fríos del mundo.

[1 mark]

1 1 . 2   Siempre he querido salvar a las aves que están en peligro.

[1 mark]

1 1 . 3   He trabajado de bombero y quiero apagar fuegos.

[1 mark]

1 1 . 4   Quiero ayudar a los ciudadanos que no tienen agua en la capital.

[1 mark]

| 1 | 2 |

Excursiones escolares

Tus compañeros españoles describen sus experiencias en las excursiones de este año.

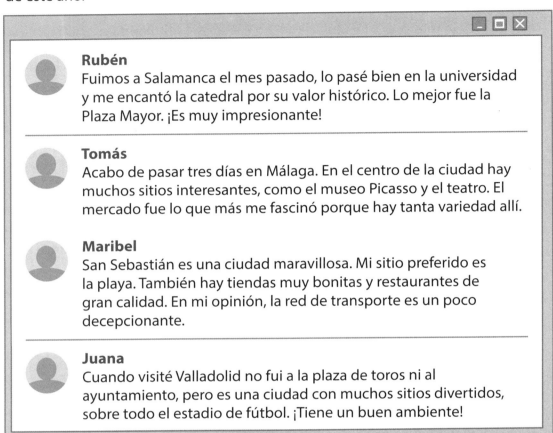

Rubén
Fuimos a Salamanca el mes pasado, lo pasé bien en la universidad y me encantó la catedral por su valor histórico. Lo mejor fue la Plaza Mayor. ¡Es muy impresionante!

Tomás
Acabo de pasar tres días en Málaga. En el centro de la ciudad hay muchos sitios interesantes, como el museo Picasso y el teatro. El mercado fue lo que más me fascinó porque hay tanta variedad allí.

Maribel
San Sebastián es una ciudad maravillosa. Mi sitio preferido es la playa. También hay tiendas muy bonitas y restaurantes de gran calidad. En mi opinión, la red de transporte es un poco decepcionante.

Juana
Cuando visité Valladolid no fui a la plaza de toros ni al ayuntamiento, pero es una ciudad con muchos sitios divertidos, sobre todo el estadio de fútbol. ¡Tiene un buen ambiente!

¿Cuál es el lugar **favorito** de cada estudiante?

Ejemplo   Ruben

la Plaza Mayor

| 1 | 2 | . | 1 | Tomás

[1 mark]

1 2 . 2   Maribel

_____

_____

[1 mark]

1 2 . 3   Juana

_____

_____

[1 mark]

| 1 | 3 |

Padres e hijos: las relaciones

Ves esta página en una revista sobre las relaciones familiales. Tres expertos dan su opinión.

Experto A	Muchos padres no tienen buenas relaciones con sus hijos adolescentes. En general, esto es debido a la falta de comunicación. La solución más fácil es tener tiempo para hablar. Lo que sugiero firmemente es comer juntos; compartir una comida deliciosa es la excusa perfecta para hablar sobre temas problemáticos.
Experto B	Los adolescentes siempre evitan hablar con sus padres sobre el instituto o sus amigos. Por eso, recomiendo a los padres que siempre hablen con sus hijos mientras hacen las tareas del hogar. A veces, cocinar juntos el fin de semana es una buena ocasión para hablar.
Experto C	Un problema muy común es cuando los hijos quieren salir con sus amigos y volver tarde por la noche. ¿Cuál es la hora ideal para volver? Depende de la circunstancia, pero los padres deberían dialogar y decidir sobre los horarios con sus hijos.

¿Cuál de los expertos expresa cada opinión?

Escribe la letra correcta en la casilla.

| 1 | 3 |.| 1 | Es una buena idea compartir los quehaceres.

[1 mark]

| 1 | 3 |.| 2 | Es recomendable almorzar en familia.

[1 mark]

| 1 | 3 |.| 3 | Puedes preparar algo rico con tu hijo.

[1 mark]

| 1 | 3 |.| 4 | Hay que tomar juntos una decisión sobre cuándo regresar a casa.

[1 mark]

| 1 | 4 |

Ofertas de empleo

Ves estas ofertas de empleo en una página web española.

¿A qué trabajo se refieren?

A	Cartero
B	Profesor
C	Recepcionista
D	Azafata
E	Pastelero

Escribe la letra correcta en cada casilla.

| 1 | 4 | . | 1 |

Empleo disponible para personas con experiencia en la enseñanza. Importante ser paciente y hablar dos idiomas.

[1 mark]

| 1 | 4 | . | 2 |

Trabajo a partir de octubre.
Llamadas de clientes, reservas de habitaciones y organización de reuniones.

[1 mark]

| 1 | 4 | . | 3 |

Empleo a tiempo parcial en nuestra tienda principal. Indispensable tener conocimientos de repostería, dulces tradicionales y modernos.

[1 mark]

1 5 | Consejos para llevar una vida sana

Lees estas ideas en una revista peruana.

Para llevar la vida más sana . . .

1. No eliminar la merienda. Es importante no ignorar el hambre.

2. Consumir 2 litros de líquidos al día, preferentemente agua.

3. Dormir al menos ocho horas al día.

4. Evitar la ansiedad practicando respiración controlada.

A	Hidratación
B	Estrés
C	Ejercicio
D	Comida
E	Sueño

Escribe la letra correcta en cada casilla.

1 5 . 1 Idea (1) [ ] **[1 mark]**

1 5 . 2 Idea (2) [ ] **[1 mark]**

1 5 . 3 Idea (3) [ ] **[1 mark]**

1 5 . 4 Idea (4) [ ] **[1 mark]**

Section C   Translation into **English**

| 1 | 6 |

You have just read this social media post from a Spanish friend.

Translate it into **English** for your family.

> Pienso que la televisión no es tan popular hoy en día. Mi hermano y yo solo vemos dramas históricos y partidos de fútbol en casa de vez en cuando. Ayer mi madre descargó un programa sobre la moda española. Este fin de semana vamos a ir al teatro.

[9 marks]

_____

_____

_____

_____

_____

_____

_____

_____

_____

_____

_____

_____

END OF QUESTIONS

Answers and mark schemes

Foundation Tier Paper 4 Writing

Time allowed: 1 hour

Instructions

- You must answer **four** questions.
- You must answer Question 1, Question 2 and Question 3.
- You must answer **either** Question 4.1 **or** Question 4.2. Do not answer **both** of these questions.
- Answer all questions in **Spanish**.
- Answer the questions in the spaces provided.
- Cross through any work you do not want to be marked.

Information

- The marks for the questions are shown in brackets.
- The maximum mark for this paper is 50.
- You must **not** use a dictionary during this test.
- In order to score the highest marks for Question 4.1/Question 4.2, you must write something about each bullet point. You must use a variety of vocabulary and structures and include your opinions.

Please note: The Practice Paper questions and answers have not been written or approved by AQA.

| 0 | 1 |

Answer the questions in the spaces provided.

Decides compartir esta foto en WhatsApp con un amigo argentino.

¿Qué hay en la foto? Escribe **cuatro** frases en **español**.

| 0 | 1 | . | 1 |

_____

[2 marks]

| 0 | 1 | . | 2 |

_____

[2 marks]

| 0 | 1 | . | 3 |

_____

[2 marks]

| 0 | 1 | . | 4 |

_____

[2 marks]

0	2

Un estudiante chileno, Marcelo, te ha preguntado sobre ti y tu familia.

Escríbele un email.

Menciona:

- tu aspecto físico

- tu carácter

- tu relación con un miembro de tu familia

- tus amigos.

Escribe aproximadamente **40** palabras en **español**.

[16 marks]

_____

_____

_____

_____

_____

_____

_____

_____

_____

_____

_____

_____

_____

_____

_____

_____

| 0 | 3 |

Translate the following sentences into **Spanish**.

I like to drink sparkling water.

_____

_____

My uncle is very chatty.

_____

_____

She lives in a modern house.

_____

_____

I bought a new jacket on Saturday.

_____

_____

I would like to learn French and Italian next year.

_____

_____

[10 marks]

Answer **either** Question 4.1 **or** Question 4.2.
You must **not** answer **both** of these questions.

EITHER Question 4.1

| 0 | 4 | . | 1 | Escribes un blog para un colegio español sobre el uso de Internet en tu país.

Menciona:

- cómo usaste Internet el fin de semana pasado

- tu opinión sobre los peligros de Internet

- cómo vas a usar Internet para preparar tus próximos exámenes

- tu aparato electrónico favorito.

Escribe aproximadamente **90** palabras en **español**. Responde a todos los aspectos de la pregunta.

[16 marks]

Or Question 4.2

| 0 | 4 | . | 2 | Tu amigo ecuatoriano te manda un email y te pregunta sobre tu instituto.

Responde a su email.

Menciona:

- qué hiciste en el instituto el viernes pasado

- tu opinión sobre las instalaciones

- qué asignaturas te gustan más

- qué vas a hacer el año que viene.

Escribe aproximadamente **90** palabras en **español**. Responde a todos los aspectos de la pregunta.

[16 marks]

END OF QUESTIONS

Model answers and mark schemes

Great Clarendon Street, Oxford, OX2 6DP, United Kingdom

Oxford University Press is a department of the University of Oxford.

It furthers the University's objective of excellence in research, scholarship, and education by publishing worldwide. Oxford is a registered trade mark of Oxford University Press in the UK and in certain other countries

British Library Cataloguing in Publication Data
Data available

978-1-38-200703-0

10 9 8 7 6 5 4 3 2 1

Paper used in the production of this book is a natural, recyclable product made from wood grown in sustainable forests. The manufacturing process conforms to the environmental regulations of the country of origin.

Printed in Great Britain by Ashford Colour Press Ltd, Gosport.

Acknowledgements
Cover illustrations: vectoriart/iStockphoto

The publisher and authors would like to thank the following for permission to use photographs and other copyright material:

Photos: p21: fizkes/Shutterstock; **p22:** BlueOrange Studio/Shutterstock; **p23:** Monkey Business Images/Shutterstock; **p50:** leoks/Shutterstock; **p69:** SpeedKingz/Shutterstock; **p70:** Pressmaster/Shutterstock; **p71:** Friends Stock/Shutterstock; **p96:** New Africa/Shutterstock; **p117:** Halfpoint/Shutterstock; **p118:** wavebreakmedia/Shutterstock; **p119:** Christian Martinez/Dreamstime; **p146:** Photographee.eu/ Shutterstock.

Although we have made every effort to trace and contact all copyright holders before publication this has not been possible in all cases. If notified, the publisher will rectify any errors or omissions at the earliest opportunity.

Links to third party websites are provided by Oxford in good faith and for information only. Oxford disclaims any responsibility for the materials contained in any third party website referenced in this work.